INTENDED
FOR GOOD

God's sovereign rule is complicated but crucial. Melvin Tinker steers us through with clarity and thoughtfulness, always keeping himself to what the Bible actually says rather than what we might want it to say. That faithfulness to Scripture, combined with pastoral sensitivity and application to life, makes this a most welcome and useful book.

Graham Beynon, Grace Church, Cambridge, director of Training for East Anglia Ministry

'Is anybody in charge around here?' 'Does anybody care about me?' The answer to both these questions is 'God', and that is the Christian doctrine of providence. In this easy-to-read book, Melvin Tinker brings home to us what that means in practice as we see God working out his purposes in our lives. There are no simple answers, but Revd Tinker can make hard things clear and help us to understand who is watching over us and why. Highly recommended.

Gerald Bray, Research Professor, Beeson Divinity School; author of The Doctrine of God

Melvin Tinker has the gift of making difficult doctrines accessible. Here he does it with the 'mystery' of the Bible's teaching on providence. There is no dumbing down, nor going further than the Bible itself takes us, in order to make matters simpler than they are. So *Intended for Good* deserves a big welcome!

Paul Helm, Teaching Fellow, Regent College, Vancouver; author of The Providence of God

ivp

MELVIN TINKER

INTENDED FOR GOOD

THE PROVIDENCE OF GOD

FOREWORD BY D. A. CARSON

APOLLOS (an imprint of Inter-Varsity Press)
Norton Street, Nottingham NG7 3HR, England
Email: ivp@ivpbooks.com
Website: www.ivpbooks.com

First published 2012

British Library Cataloguing in Publication Data
A catalogue record for this book is available from the British Library.

ISBN: 978-1-84474-570-8

Set in Monotype Garamond 11/14pt
Typeset in Great Britain by CRB Associates, Potterhanworth, Lincolnshire
Printed and bound in Great Britain by Ashford Colour Press Ltd, Gosport,
Hampshire

To
Shirley Godbold
fellow worker and friend

CONTENTS

FOREWORD

Fewer than two hundred years ago, a student writing an advanced paper in most history departments in British or American universities might well include some reflections on what his or her historical treatment implied about divine providence. Today it is unthinkable to include such reflection. At a more mundane level, reflections on divine providence continue to surface in trivial conversations. Not long ago I was flying home after speaking at a conference somewhere, and it appeared that our plane was going be delayed by an hour or two because of bad weather, or perhaps forced to land at another airport. Suddenly the pilot announced that there was a small break in the weather, and we were heading straight in with minimal delay. The passenger in the next seat smiled and muttered, 'Someone up there loves me: I'll make my connecting flight.' I confess I smiled back and asked him, 'If you missed your flight, would that constitute evidence that he doesn't love you?'

Three and a half centuries ago, it was not uncommon for Christians to muse on 'the mystery of providence'. Our contemporary lack of reflection on this theme overlooks how important it is in the Bible – and we abandon it at our peril. The reason the doctrine of providence is mysterious lies in the fact that it brings together God's utter sovereignty and his unqualified goodness. On the one hand,

God truly reigns: the world never escapes from his ultimate control. Yet if that is the only thing to be said, one risks giving the impression that God stands symmetrically behind good and evil – and that would make him amoral. But the same Bible that affirms God's sovereignty insists equally on God's goodness: he reigns providentially.

Sometimes the biblical texts lift the veil just a little, to indicate some of the ways this is so. The Assyrians slaughter Israelites and grind them into the mud, a barbarous regional superpower intoxicated by its own military prowess – yet unknown to them, God is actually using them to bring judgment on his people, deploying the Assyrians as a man wields an axe or some other tool, and he will in turn hold the Assyrians accountable for their attitude (Isa. 10:5–19). Whether an individual Israelite escapes or is cut down in the vicious slaughter, that Israelite lives and perhaps dies under the providence of God. Wicked leaders conspire to pervert justice and execute Jesus, and clearly they are accountable for their sins, yet from another perspective they did nothing more than what God ordained should be done, for otherwise one must read the cross of Christ as little more than an accident of history (Acts 4:27–28).

So now we are holding together three strands of biblical evidence: God's sovereignty, God's goodness and human accountability. Each of these strands is very common in Scripture, and raises a plethora of questions about time and eternity, the nature of what philosophers call 'secondary causality', and, at the personal level, anguished despair when things seem so unfair (think Job and Ps. 88). The question is how these themes hold together, and how they should be applied to life and history, such that we avoid, on the one hand, a Mary Poppins view of reality, and, on the other, robotic fatalism ('Que sera, sera!' What will be, will be!), while maintaining resilient faith in the manifold perfections of God and an awareness of our own need of grace.

In this book Melvin Tinker takes on these broad themes and strives for biblical faithfulness. Equally, he shows how the doctrine of providence ought to function in a believer's life: this book is pastorally shrewd and sensitive. It will not answer all our questions (I'm not sure all our questions will be answered even in the new heaven and the new earth), but it will provide a framework of mature Christian reflection that will stabilize us as we focus with joy and trust on God's perfections and reliability.

D. A. Carson

ACKNOWLEDGEMENTS

The Puritans used to say that 'providence is the last refuge of the saints'. Over recent years both my own personal experience and work as a pastor has led me to believe that the doctrine of God's providence should be amongst the first refuges a Christian should seek in order to find strength and comfort. It has to be admitted that the belief in God's providence has fallen upon hard times. In the early church (especially in the writings of Chrysostom) right through into the early part of the nineteenth century, providence was part of the staple diet of professing Christians. For various reasons, the doctrine was eclipsed in the twentieth century and still lies on the edges of much Christian thought and practice today. This is a great pity. Rightly understood, providence shines as a glorious jewel in the crown of the Christian faith. This book is a modest attempt to explore many of the wonderful facets of that jewel in a way which is pastoral and practical.

I would like to thank the faculty of Trinity Evangelical Divinity School, Deerfield, Illinois, for their kind assistance and the use of their excellent facilities in the writing of this book. In particular, I would like to express my deepest appreciation to Dr D. A. Carson and his delightful wife, Joy, who showed nothing but immense kindness in their hospitality to my wife and I during our happy stay at Deerfield.

I would also like to express my thanks to Shirley Godbold for her diligent proof-reading of the first drafts of the book and her constant loyalty and support. I am especially grateful to Philip Tinker for not only checking the manuscripts, but also for making many helpful comments along the way and providing the questions for reflection and discussion. As always, his sharp and perceptive mind, as well as his graciousness, has been of great benefit to me throughout this project. I am also grateful for the comments by an anonymous reader who assessed an early draft for IVP.

I thank God that in his providence he has led me to pastor a church which delights in God's word and seeks to live in its light. I am grateful to St John, Newland for allowing me an extended study leave in which to write this book. Thanks are also in order to the staff team of St John's, especially my associate colleagues, Lee McMunn, Scott McKay and Jake Belder, who took up much of the ministerial slack in my absence.

Finally, I wish to thank my wife, Heather, for her continued support and encouragement. She still remains my best critic and dearest friend.

Soli Deo gloria
Melvin Tinker, 2011

1. PROVIDENCE AND THE PURPOSES OF GOD (Romans 8:28)

One of the most well-loved hymns of an earlier generation is, 'God moves in a mysterious way':

> God moves in a mysterious way
>   His wonders to perform;
> He plants His footsteps in the sea,
>   And rides upon the storm.
>
> Deep in unfathomable mines
>   Of never-failing skill,
> He treasures up His bright designs
>   And works His sovereign will.
>
> Ye fearful saints, fresh courage take;
>   The clouds you so much dread
> Are big with mercy, and shall break
>   In blessings on your head.

Judge not the Lord by feeble sense,
　　But trust Him for His grace;
Behind a frowning providence
　　He hides a smiling face.

His purposes will ripen fast,
　　Unfolding every hour;
The bud may have a bitter taste,
　　But sweet will be the flower.

Blind unbelief is sure to err,
　　And scan his work in vain;
God is his own interpreter,
　　And He will make it plain.

The hymn was written by William Cowper on 1st January 1773. What many people don't realize is that earlier that morning he was walking in a field near Olney, where he lived, when he had a terrible premonition that a curse of madness was going to fall upon him. He had been plagued with mental problems before. Struggling to make a declaration of his Christian faith in poetic form before the cloud of depression engulfed his mind (he was a first-class poet), he struggled home, picked up his pen and wrote that magnificent hymn. It was soon after he had finished writing that Cowper's mind plunged into the abyss of a complete mental breakdown. During the night he had terrible dreams and hallucinations; in one fit of madness he believed that he had received God's command to take his own life with a knife, similar to the way Abraham was called to sacrifice his son Isaac. Amazingly the suicide attempt was thwarted by a Christian friend, Mary Unwin, who in the small hours of the morning sent for Cowper's local vicar and friend, another hymn writer, John Newton of 'Amazing Grace' fame. When Newton found him, Cowper's body was a bloody mess but thankfully his suicide attempt had not been fatal. Throughout the following weeks, day after day, night after night, Newton tried to calm and console his troubled

friend. This went on for four months until April when C
some measure of recovery, which sadly, was never to b
In August of 1775, three years later, Newton describe
mental illness as, 'mysterious . . . a very great trial to me. But I hope
I am learning (though I am a slow student) to silence all vain reason-
ings and unbelieving complaints with the consideration of the Lord's
sovereignty, wisdom and love'.[1]

What was it that enabled John Newton to write those words and
Cowper his hymn? It was the steadying belief expressed in these
famous words of the apostle Paul: 'And we know that in all things
God works for the good of those who love him, who have been
called according to his purpose' (Rom. 8:28). We might ask: 'Is Paul
really serious in saying that God is working for the good of those
who love him *in all* things, even the hard and painful things?' Most
certainly, which is why Paul wrote these words at this point in his
letter, because a few verses earlier he had been talking about the
whole of creation groaning because of the corrosive effects of sin,
and a few verses later he will speak of Christians suffering persecu-
tion and famine and yet conclude, 'in all these things we are more
than conquerors through him who loved us' (v. 37) and that nothing
in heaven or on earth or in hell 'will be able to separate us from the
love of God that is in Christ Jesus our Lord' (v. 39).

A basis for confidence

We may be minded to ask: why should Paul and all Christians have
such confidence? The answer is because of the power and purposes
of God which come together in the doctrine of providence. In the
Bible God presents himself from beginning to end as the one who
is in complete personal control of *every* detail of human existence.
Here it is, for example, in Isaiah 45:6–7: 'I am the LORD, and there
is no other. I form the light and create darkness, I bring prosperity
and create disaster; I, the LORD, do all these things.' God is involved
in the macro level of world politics, which is what Isaiah refers to

earlier in the chapter when speaking of God raising up King Cyrus (who at the time of writing was not even born), to bring down Babylon which was about to take God's people into captivity. Cyrus was to be God's servant (pagan though he was) in setting God's people free.

But God is also at work at the micro level too, such that he personally determines the lifespan of a single sparrow according to the teaching of Jesus: 'Are not two sparrows sold for a penny? Yet not one of them will fall to the ground apart from the will of your Father. And even the very hairs of your head are numbered' (Matt. 10:29–30). God is concerned with that amount of detail! However, we are not to envisage that this is the obsessive concern of a celestial busybody, because Jesus goes on to say to his followers, 'So don't be afraid; *you* are worth more than many sparrows.' This is a very practical teaching which is meant to comfort and encourage God's people, *especially* for when the tough times come our way. After all, Jesus says that the God who is all powerful, all wise and all good is the one we can call 'Father'.[2]

The doctrine of providence is a subset of the doctrine of God's sovereignty which Bruce Ware defines in these terms: 'God exhaustively plans and meticulously carries out his perfect will as he alone knows best, regarding all that is in heaven and on earth, and he does so without failure or defeat, accomplishing his purposes in all of creation from the smallest details to the grand purposes of his plan for the whole of the created order.'[3] From an earlier generation, B. B. Warfield speaks of God's providential control in these terms, 'There is nothing that is, and nothing that comes to pass, that [God] has not first decreed and then brought to pass by His creation or providence.'[4]

Although we shall be focusing on the implications of providence for Christian believers, it is important to underscore the fact that by definition providence applies to all creation and all people:

Jesus himself urges us to pray for daily bread, a petition almost certainly based on his Father's providential care in daily living (especially in the wider context of Matthew 6). It does indeed seem that the activity of God is 'all in all'. There is no time or space where he is excluded, no kinds of men or society or natural phenomena which are not caught up in some way within the pervasive, perpetual and purposive motion of God.[5]

But what do Christians mean when they speak of providence? Perhaps a useful starting point would be to think of the different ways Christians tend to use the term.[6]

Providence – different meanings

Imagine that there has been a pandemic of bird flu and despite the fact that the rest of her family went down with it, Mrs Miggins didn't. Wisely she took reasonable precautions against contracting the illness; she had an inoculation, she made sure her hands were always washed (of course she had prayed about it too!). Being a Christian believer she naturally attributes the fact that she was spared to God's providence. What she means when she speaks in this way is that her *not* going down with flu was a good thing and it was *God* who had made sure she hadn't contracted it. To be sure, this still leaves us with the issue as to what God was doing with those who *did* go down with flu, but we shall come back to that question in a moment. We can put it like this: Mrs Miggins believes that it is not the devil that is in the detail, but God who is sovereignly bringing about his good purposes for his people, 'providing' or 'governing' if you will. That is providence.

Imagine another situation. Bob Bates is a salesman. He too is a Christian but has been finding life to be something of a struggle for him recently. The economic downturn has not been too kind to his business and he is a hairsbreadth away from insolvency. To add insult to injury he just misses his train to London for an important business appointment which he hoped would land him a good order. To make things really miserable it begins to rain. However, it so happens that

Bob bumps into an old school friend he hasn't seen for years who, unlike himself, has done quite well in the business world. As a result of this 'chance' meeting, his friend places a large order for Bob's products. What does Bob conclude? Like Mrs Miggins, Bob is a Christian and so reflects on the matter biblically and comes to the happy conclusion that it was 'providential' that he missed the train because if he had caught it, he wouldn't have met his friend and in turn he wouldn't have bagged the order which put his business back on its feet.

From one point of view, to say that God is providentially at work in all things may mean no more than whatever happens, happens by divine say-so. This means that even falling off the pavement, which at one level can be described as an 'accident' because of a loose slab, at another (higher) level can be conceived as being within the orbit of God's personal ruling decree. However, what we normally mean when we speak of something being 'providential' is that we perceive an event or series of happenings to be *significant*, we believe that we can see some sort of divine pattern or purpose in them: Mrs Miggins being kept healthy to care for her sick family, Bob Bates being provided for his business and so on. Accordingly, we might define providence as: *God our heavenly Father working in and through all things by his wisdom and power for the good of his people and the glory of his name.*

Much of what we call 'providence' is considered with hindsight, that is, it is retrospective. Sometimes things happen to us and while they are happening we haven't a clue as to their significance; it is only months, or sometimes years, later that we can look back and say, 'Now I see; *that* is what God was doing.' The other reason why we have not to be too quick in deciding whether an occurrence is providential or not in an immediately good sense is because things might turn out rather differently as time goes by. For example, let's imagine that Bob Bates as a result of his business deal with his friend decides, unwisely as it turns out, to expand his business. In fact he over-expands, with the result that he becomes bankrupt. If that happens he might be less eager to call his chance meeting with his friend at the train station providential. But then again that is not necessarily the end of the story. Let us further imagine that as a result of his bankruptcy he goes on to gain a better perspective on life, with the result that he no longer spends all his waking hours at work, trying to make more and more money. Indeed, he now begins to spend more time with his family who up to this point have seen very little of him. What is more, Bob gets involved in the children's work at his local church which has been desperate for a male worker for years. At this juncture Bob reflects on all that has happened and gladly attributes it all to the providence of God.

This relates to another aspect of providence, what can be called the 'preventative hand' of providence. This is the understanding that God sometimes prevents untoward things happening which are unbeknown to us. However, we may discover God's protective care in such cases at a later time. An example of this aspect of providence is an incident which occurred during the American Civil War.[7] Levi Hefner, a Confederate courier, was sent one night by his command-ing officer, General Robert E. Lee, to take a message through an area partially occupied by Union troops. As he approached a bridge, his horse balked and reared nervously. Hefner dismounted and attempted to calm him. In the darkness he began singing softly a familiar hymn, 'Jesus, Lover of My Soul', and in a few minutes the horse became quiet. Hefner then mounted his horse, crossed the bridge without incident and completed his mission. A number of years after the war, Hefner attended a reunion of soldiers from both sides of the conflict. As they gathered in small groups to share experiences they remembered from the war, a Union soldier from Ohio recounted standing guard one dark night at a bridge, having been ordered to shoot anyone approaching from the other side. During the night only one rider came his way, and so he raised his rifle to shoot as soon as he could see the form in the darkness. Just then, however, the horse balked and the rider dismounted. To calm the horse, the rider began singing softly a hymn, 'Jesus, Lover of My Soul'. The Union soldier told the circle of old soldiers that the sound of the hymn so touched him that he lowered his rifle and quietly turned away. He said, 'I could not shoot him.' Levi Hefner jumped up and embraced the Union soldier, saying, 'That was me!' He realized for the first time that his singing that dark night had saved his life, or from another standpoint, God had saved it.

Principles in understanding providence

There are three important principles which come into play when we think about providence and how we might begin to understand it.

First, we need to identify properly the good purpose that *God* has in mind. Paul says, 'In all things God works for the *good* for those who love him, who have been called according to his purpose'. It is what *God* considers to be 'good' rather than what *we* think is good that matters. This is not a text for the Prosperity Gospel: 'Have faith and God will bless you with riches and a happy and trouble-free life.' It is important to look very carefully at what Paul says next: 'For those God foreknew he also predestined *to be conformed to the likeness of his Son*.' Now we can see clearly what God's good purpose is – it is to be made more like Jesus, having a practical conformity to Christ. Mrs Miggins was spared the flu *so that* she could show kindness and love, just like Jesus. Bill Bates learnt his lesson from his greed and adjusted his priorities *so that* he would be like Jesus in 'seeking first the kingdom of heaven'.

This also helps towards answering the question: 'What about those in the family who did become ill with the flu?' It could be reasoned that they *had to* go down with the flu and Mrs Miggins spared, if she was to be in a position to care for them and so become more like Christ (in this context this is what is known as a 'necessary condition'). What is more, this was an opportunity for the rest of the family to perhaps take stock of what really matters, maybe to appreciate God's blessings of good health in the light of its absence as well as the kindness of God shown through Mrs Miggins. The point is this: whether easy times or hard times come our way, God will use them to shape us so that we become little mirror images of his Son.

Secondly, how God will work providentially so that we become more like Jesus will to some degree depend upon our *response* to what happens to us. This is not fatalism – we are not talking about 'whatever will be will be' – because human choices are involved, which God is involved in too. Again going back to our two examples, Mrs Miggins *could* have taken her escaping the flu as an opportunity to be selfish. She might have said, 'Let the family fend for itself, I am taking a holiday in Spain until all of this blows over.' Bob Bates *might* have responded to his loss of his business with cynicism and resentment, throwing in the towel with the cry, 'Why has God done this to me?' But instead both chose to respond *positively in obedient faith.* They knew God's commands: love your neighbour as yourself, seek first the kingdom of God, and so they decided with the help of God's Spirit to obey him.

Thirdly, we have to have a proper perspective, which is the *long-term view*. Being made more like Jesus is a lifetime's work God *eternity* does within us. So we are not always able to discern a providential pattern *straight away*. In fact we have to admit that in this life we may not be able to discern much of a pattern at all in some of the things which happen to us. Some lives, including some Christian ones, seemed marked by very little else but pointlessness and tragedy, the stuff of the book of Ecclesiastes: 'Vanity, vanity, all is vanity' (as the King James version puts it), words written by a believer.[8] The pain being borne by someone might be such that, to be frank, it is very difficult for a person to reflect calmly and rationally upon what is happening to them and the ones they love. What are they to do then, when their world seems to be falling apart? That is when in the teeth of the evidence they hold on to what Paul teaches in Romans 8, that God is still our Father, that he is still on the throne and that he is working all things for the good of those who love him.[9]

I know a minister who many years ago was involved in a terrible car accident in which his young wife died. He himself was seriously injured and had to have extensive surgery to rebuild his face. He asked his own minister at the time what he could possibly do, how on earth was he ever going to retrieve his life after this? And very gently, but with a quiet conviction, the minister wisely told him to keep on reading Romans 8:28 over and over to himself until he really believed it. He did just that. Eventually he remarried and now has a family and fruitful Christian ministry.

Sometimes, however, we may be able to see something of the 'good' of which Paul speaks in *this* life. One of the most influential evangelical scholars of the post-war era was John Wenham. He too was involved in a car accident when he was quite advanced in years and in the event his wife died. The remarkable thing that happened afterwards was this: he found himself in hospital in the same ward as the very driver who had caused the accident which killed his wife. Did Wenham take this as an opportunity to vent his spleen with the man who had caused him so much grief? Not at all, instead he led the man to a personal faith in Jesus Christ. John Wenham really did believe that in all things God works for the good of those who love him. This is what Cowper means by the line, 'Behind a frowning providence He hides a *smiling* face'.

One more moving example of the providential care of God which is both hard and hopeful is that of Adoniram Judson.

Adoniram Judson was the first American overseas missionary who in 1813 at the age of twenty-four went with his twenty-three-year old wife to Burma. He worked there for thirty-eight years until his death at the age of sixty-one, having had only one trip home after thirty-three years in the mission field. All his years in Burma were hard but the early years especially so. For example, Ann, who married Judson on 5 February 1812, bore three children to Adoniram. All of them died. The first baby, nameless, was born dead just as they sailed from India to Burma. The second child, Roger Williams Judson, lived seventeen months and died. The third, Maria Elizabeth Butterworth Judson, lived to be two, and outlived her mother by six months and then died. Adoniram eventually married three times, with two of his wives dying on the mission field. It was six years before they saw their first convert. The years after that first convert were very hard indeed. On 8 June 1824 Adoniram was dragged from his home and put in prison. His feet were fettered and at night a long horizontal bamboo pole was lowered and passed between his legs and hoisted up until only his shoulders and head rested on the ground. Ann at the time was pregnant, but walked the two miles daily to the palace to plead that Judson was not a Western spy and that he should be shown mercy. She got some relief for him so that he could come out into a courtyard. But still the prisoners found lice in their hair and had to be shaved bald. Almost a year later, they were suddenly moved to a more distant village prison looking gaunt, with hollow eyes, dressed in rags and crippled from the torture. There the mosquitoes from the rice paddies on their bloody feet almost drove them mad. The daughter, Maria, had by now been born and Ann was sick and thin, but still followed after Adoniram with her baby in order to take care of him as best she could. Her milk dried up, and the jailer had mercy on them and actually let Adoniram take the baby each evening into the village and beg for women to nurse his baby. On 4 November 1825, Judson was suddenly released. Apparently, the government needed him as a translator in their negotiations with Britain. The long ordeal was over – seventeen months in prison and on the brink of death, with his wife sacrificing herself and her baby to care for him, Ann's health was broken. Eleven months later she died. Six months later their daughter died. But in 1831 something began to happen and God was suddenly moving in a very powerful way. Judson wrote:

> The spirit of inquiry . . . is spreading everywhere, through the whole length and breadth of the land. [We have distributed] nearly 10,000 tracts, giving to none but those who ask. I presume there have been 6,000 applications at the house. Some come two or three months' journey, from the borders of Siam and China: 'Sir, we hear that there is an eternal hell. We are afraid of it. Do give us a writing that will tell us how to escape it.' Others, from the frontiers of Kathay, 100 miles north of Ava: 'Sir, we have seen a writing that tells about an eternal God. Are you the man that gives away such writings? If so, pray give us one, for we want to know the truth before we die.' Others, from the

interior of the country, where the name of Jesus Christ is a little known: 'Are you Jesus Christ's man? Give us a writing that tells us about Jesus Christ.'

That was two hundred years ago. Now there are two million Christian believers in that country and 40% of the Karen people, who were the folk Judson primarily worked amongst, are followers of the Lord Jesus Christ.[10]

While it is sometimes said that Christians believe that there are no such things as 'accidents' only 'God incidents', so that every single event has meaning within the great scheme of things, the real significance and purpose of some events may not be seen in this life at all, but only in eternity, which, after all, is the fuller setting of God's big picture.

How might we understand how this works out? Here is a simple illustration. It is said that Persian carpets are made on a large frame. On one side of the frame stand the mother and her children, placing different coloured threads into the framework, sometimes randomly, sometimes thoughtfully. On the other side of the frame out of sight stands the father of the family. He is the master carpet weaver who takes all of these threads and weaves them into a rich pattern of *his* design. As the work is in progress, all that the family can see from their side of the frame are rough patterns, and in some cases, no pattern at all. But from the father's side he knows *exactly* what he is doing with the threads his family put into the frame. When the carpet is completed the father turns the finished product around for all to see and hopefully receives their approval of a job well done. Might not God, the Heavenly Father, be likened to the master weaver who takes each thread that we place into the framework of our lives only to weave them into a pattern which is of his design? The main difference being, of course, is that from the beginning God knows what those threads are and where they will be placed on 'our' side of the frame. However, it is the 'other' side of the frame, eternity if you will, which provides the lasting context in which ultimate significance is derived. It is in the new heaven and the new earth that we will be able to declare that our God has done all things well. We hold to that now by faith, then it will give way to sight.[11]

The comforting teaching of providence has been well put by Dr Broughton Knox:

> The doctrine of God's absolute and complete providence and control over every event is a ground for banishing fear from the hearts of the people of God. Thus Jesus reminded his disciples, 'Are not five sparrows sold for two pennies? And yet not one of them is forgotten by God. Indeed the very hairs of your head are all numbered. Do not fear; for you are of more value than many sparrows.' In the Old Testament the doctrine of God's sovereignty is the comfort and strength of his people. Thus through the prophet Isaiah God says, 'I even I, am he that comforts you. Who are you that you are afraid of man who dies, and of the son of man who is made like grass; that you have forgotten Yahweh your Maker, who stretched out the heavens and laid the foundations of the earth.' The creative power of God which brought all things into being is the guarantee that he is able to sustain us in every detail of life . . . The infinite power and infinite mind of God, to which the marvels of creation bear witness, mean that he is able to give full attention, care and protection to every person in the world with the same intensity of concern that he would give if he were related to a single individual only. The infinity of God is not overwhelmed by numbers, nor stupefied by detail. God is able to comprehend, and provide for at the same time, the needs of the whole creation. Our heavenly Father gives each of us his undivided attention and his full friendship as though we were his only friend.[12]

Questions for reflection and discussion

1. What examples of God's providence can you see in your life like that of Mrs Miggins (providence in the detail) and Bob Bates (the big picture)?

2. How does God's purpose for your life (Rom. 8:29) compare with your priorities and ambitions?

3. 'The doctrine of God's absolute and complete providence and control over every event is a ground for banishing fear from the hearts of the people of God.' What would it mean for us if God were not in complete control?

4. When you're confused about what is happening in life, what is your natural response? How should God's providence affect this?

Notes

1. See Jonathan Aitken, *John Newton* (Continuum Press, 2007), pp. 155–160.

2. Here is just a sample of biblical texts which relate to God's sovereignty over all things: the entire universe (Ps. 103:19; Rom. 8:28; Eph. 1:11), all of nature (Ps. 135:6–7; Matt. 5:45; 6:25–30), angels and even Satan (Ps. 103:20–21; Job 1:12), all of the nations (Ps. 47:7–9; Dan. 2:20–21; 4:34–35), every human person and his/her choices (Exod. 3:21; 12:26–36; 1 Sam. 2:6–8; Ezra 7:27; Gal. 1:15–16), every animal and its choices (Ps. 104:21–30; 1 Kgs 17:4–6), all events that appear to be 'accidental' (Prov. 16:33; Jon. 1:7; Luke 12:6), all the sinful acts of man and Satan (Gen 45:5; 50:20; 2 Sam. 24:1; 1 Chr. 21:1). For a thorough and judicious presentation of the biblical material, see Steven C. Roy, *How Much Does God Foreknow? A Comprehensive Biblical Study* (Apollos, 2006).

3. Bruce Ware, 'Prayer and the Sovereignty of God', in Sam Storms and Justin Taylor (eds.), *For the Fame of God's Name – Essays in Honour of John Piper* (Crossway, 2010), p. 128.

4. Cited by Paul Helseth, 'God Causes All Things', in Dennis W. Jowers (ed.), *Four Views on Divine Providence* (Zondervan, 2011), p. 27.

5. Vernon White, *The Fall of a Sparrow: A Concept of Special Divine Action* (Paternoster, 1985), p. 36.

6. This is a development of an illustration suggested by Paul Helm, in *The Providence of God* (Inter-Varsity Press, 1993).

7. I owe this example to Dr Dale Ralph Davies.

8. The word translated 'vanity' or 'meaningless' is *hebel*, which conveys the notion of something being transitory or insubstantial. It has been suggested that it is translated 'bubbles'– that is what life *feels* like 'under the sun' (Eccl. 1:2–3).

9. 'Even the best insights of faith will not give us the whole picture correctly. It is part of the meaning of faith that it does not. We will often have to appeal to, and trust, the wider context and configuration of ends and events, without being able to see it. That appeal is the only way we can begin to cope with the "sickening and cumulative force" of the contrary experiences, the other side of the riddle which is both the banality of life and its horror . . . Occasionally it is given us to see what is happening, and rejoice, for this is part of the riddle too. There are luminous moments, big or small, moments when an end of God is brought so compellingly to our attention in a particular event here and now, that we *know* . . . This can be as trivial as finding a lost memento after an "arrow prayer", or as crucial as the healing of a terminal illness' (White, *Fall of a Sparrow*, p. 178).

10. Sharon James, *My Heart is in His Hands – Ann Judson of Burma* (Evangelical Press, 1998).

11. For a presentation of this argument, see Melvin Tinker, *Why Do Bad Things Happen to Good People?* (Christian Focus, [5]2009).

12. D. B. Knox, *Selected Works*, vol. 1 (St Matthias Press, 2000), p. 57.

2. PROVIDENCE AND HUMAN RESPONSIBILITY

Let me make a personal confession: I dislike jigsaw puzzles. I really have no aptitude for them. My wife on the other hand, loves them. She is brilliant. She can take a puzzle of a picture of a plate of baked beans and – 'Hey presto'– it is complete in next to no time. From childhood my approach to jigsaws has always been to apply the principle of brawn over brain. If I have a piece in my hand and see a space in the puzzle which more or less looks right – in it goes! It is going to go in whether it belongs there or not – use the hammer if necessary! So what if, at the end, you have a few pieces left over? Who is to say they ever belonged to this jigsaw anyway? Maybe the manufacturers have made a mistake and put the pieces from another puzzle in the wrong box?

I would imagine that you are you are not wholly convinced by the 'Melvin Method' approach to jigsaw puzzles!

Yet this is reminiscent of how some people approach the Bible. There are those who want all the gaps in their understanding filled and therefore will attempt to force parts of the Bible's teaching together in such a way that it does violence to the overall picture. On the other hand, there are those who are not particularly enamoured with some teachings found in the Bible and would go so far as to claim they don't really belong there at all and are in effect part of another 'puzzle'. As a consequence they are conveniently put to one side.[1] However, the Bible itself would urge us to be more cautious and more patient. Knowing the temptation for God's people to do with his revelation what I tend do with jigsaws, God said through his spokesman Moses: 'The secret things belong to the LORD our God, but the things revealed belong to us and to our children forever, that we may follow all the words of his law' (Deut. 29:29). In his infinite wisdom God has chosen not to tell us every-thing we would like to know – some things are secret and known to him alone. However, God has given us enough revelation for us to trust him, which means doing what he says – '*following* the words of the law'. God has spoken not to satisfy our curiosity but to enable us to live with him faithfully. This means that the 'jigsaw' of God's word will provide a sufficient enough picture for us to trust God and, within limits, understand what he is doing and why, but *not* so much that there will never be any pieces missing. There will always be some gaps which allow for a fair degree of mystery. Accordingly, on the basis of what we *do* know we can trust God for what we *don't* know. This is called faith.

Why is such a preamble so important? It is vital because when we come to the subject of God's sovereignty exercised through providence and its relationship to human responsibility, the tempt-ation will be to move towards one of the two extremes: either to effectively deny God's sovereignty or deny human responsibility, such that the overall picture of Scripture becomes seriously distorted.[2]

The teaching found throughout the Bible declares that God is much bigger than we often imagine him to be, in that he is sovereign over every twist and turn of existence, not taking any risks, while *at the same time* recognizing that human beings are responsible for what they do. This is part of what is called the mystery of providence.

Herein lies the biblical truth that God superintends all events (including human choices) in order to fulfil a purpose of his own design. This is something the Bible presents us with without any accompanying explanation as to how God does this. The affirmation is there but not the explanation (although there are boundaries set for wrong explanations and pointers towards legitimate explanations which will, to some degree, be speculative).

Know the truth

A key truth which we are meant to grasp is that the God who is infinite, outside space and time, and so not subject to the limitations we experience, is also personally and intimately involved in space and time with the creatures he has made. He sovereignly rules over all while being God-in-relationship. We see this truth being expressed, for example, in Proverbs 16:4: 'The LORD [Yahweh] works out everything for his own ends – even the wicked for a day of disaster.' This means that the affairs and plans of men are known to him and will be used by him to serve his sovereign purpose. God is never to be found napping or caught off-guard at any point so that he is then forced to say, 'Oh dear, I didn't see that one coming. I had better revert to plan B. And if that gets messed up I will go on to plan C and work my way down.' No, his plans are never ultimately stymied by our cleverness and cunning; even wicked people come under his sovereign sway. What is more, no matter how powerful a person may be, they do not lie outside the orbit of his eternal decrees: 'The king's heart is in the hand of the LORD; he directs it like a watercourse wherever he pleases' (Prov. 21:1). The hearts of the world's movers and shakers are not no-go areas for God.

In the context of providence we are also pointed in the direction of believing that God's meticulous personal superintending covers what we might call 'chance': 'The lot is cast into the lap, but its every decision is from the LORD' (Prov. 16: 33). Sometimes 'Chance' (with a capital 'C') is put forward as an alternative causal explanation to

God. But this is really a false alternative. Chance is simply a word we use to describe events – like tossing a coin or the mutation of a gene – which either have no discernable order or no discernable cause which *we know*. This doesn't mean that such matters are not known to God. Furthermore, 'Chance' is not some metaphysical 'Other', a positive force which is to be pitted against God and so can be thought of as a God-substitute. To suppose such a thing would be to make a logical blunder. Chance is not an alternative to God – 'God or Chance'. Rather, what we call chance comes under God's care and design just as much as all the other things which we can predict more accurately like the rising and setting of the sun. He is Lord of all.[3]

Furthermore, the 'risk-free' view of providence which is being proposed here entails that there are no unforeseen by-products of God's plans. In the case of human beings such unforeseen and undesired side effects (what some might call 'collateral damage') are inevitable simply because we are locked into space and time and so not able to foresee all the consequences of our actions, although some may be anticipated. However, such limitations do not apply to God. Some writers, however, do think that God has such limitations, such that although he may want some things to happen, his plans can somehow be thrown off track by rebellious human beings and other circumstances which lie beyond his control or knowledge, with the result that he is forced to resort to altern-ative plans. Here a distinction is sometimes made between God's *antecedent* will (what he wishes to happen before an event) and his *consequent* will (what he wishes to happen in response to that event). But this can hardly be applied to the Almighty Creator who is Lord of heaven and earth. And so the philosopher, P. T. Geach rightly says, take 'the merchantman's captain who throws his wares overboard in a storm: antecedently he wills to bring them into port, consequently upon the storm he wills to throw them over-board. But the captain only does not will rather to allay the storm because this is not open to him; he is not one whom wind and sea obey'.[4]

C. S. Lewis makes a similar point,

I suggest that the distinction between plan and by-product must vanish entirely on the level of omniscience, omnipotence, and perfect goodness. I believe this because even on the human level it diminishes the higher you go. The better a human plan is made, the fewer unconsidered by-products it will have and the more birds it will kill with one stone, the more diverse needs and interests it will meet; the nearer it will come – it can never be very near – to being a plan for each individual. Bad laws make hard cases. But let us go beyond the managerial altogether. Surely a man of genius composing a poem or symphony must be less unlike God than a ruler? But the man of genius has no mere by-products in his work. Every note or word will be more than a means, more than a consequence. Nothing will be solely for the sake of other things . . . The great work of art was made for the sake of all it does and is, down to the curve of every wave and the flight of every insect.[5]

Choices, choices

However, the belief that God's sovereign rule is universal in scope is only one aspect of the biblical revelation; the complementary aspect is that human beings are responsible. We think, make decisions, and take action. Sometimes we don't think enough and still make choices – some good, some bad, some indifferent – but *we* make them as conscious agents and so are accountable to God. Just because our decisions are covered by God's will doesn't make us into puppets; puppets after all can't make decisions, human beings, however, do. Take Proverbs 16:27: 'A scoundrel plots evil, and his speech is like a scorching fire.' Why does he plot evil, using his mind to hatch some wicked scheme: pushing drugs to children, forcing women into prostitution, making a quick buck at someone else's expense? It is because he *is* a scoundrel – that is his nature. On the other hand, plotting evil *makes* him *into* a scoundrel, for this is a thinking person who is consciously engaged in plotting evil schemes.

He is responsible for doing such things and can't simply shrug his shoulders and say, 'Well, I can't help it. It is just the way I am.' He has made such choices and is responsible to God for them. Nonetheless, such choices and courses of action which are yet to be taken are not hidden from God so that he can be outsmarted or frustrated.[6]

Sometimes we find *both* divine sovereignty and human responsibility placed side by side in Scripture: 'In his heart a man plans his course [human responsibility] but the LORD determines his steps [divine sovereignty]' (Prov. 16:9). The Bible is not embarrassed in putting the two together and neither should we be.

Donald Macleod, in considering the related doctrine of fore-ordination, summarizes the relation between God's sovereignty and human freedom in the following way:

> God's fore-ordination does not eliminate human freedom. It does not take away our liberty or absolve us of responsibility for our personal actions. Judas Iscariot betrayed the Lord Jesus Christ; and he betrayed him by God's fore-ordained counsel and foreknowledge. But God also fore-ordained that Judas should betray Jesus. But God also fore-ordained that Judas should betray him freely, that he should choose to do it and that he would desire to do it. God's fore-ordination does not mean that His whole purpose moved in and forced Judas to this particular act, rather God fore-ordained that, without compulsion or coercion, Judas would freely, volitionally, and with all the moral force of his own personality, express himself in betraying the Lord Jesus Christ.[7]

Why is this teaching so important that God wants us to know about it (which is not the same as fully understanding it)? To answer that question it might be helpful to think of what happens if either of these twin truths are denied – that either God is not sovereign, but can have his plans thwarted – or that we are not responsible and are mere puppets. We need go no further than the first sermon preached on the Day of Pentecost as recorded in Acts 2:22 for the answers.

This is what the apostle Peter says:

> Men of Israel, listen to this: Jesus of Nazareth was a man accredited by
> God to you by miracles, wonders and signs, which God did among you
> through him, as you yourselves know. *This man was handed over to you by
> God's set purpose and foreknowledge; and you, with the help of wicked men, put him
> to death* by nailing him to the cross. But God raised him from the dead . . .

There is the balance. The fact is the Gospel itself is dependent upon
this tension being true.

Let us unpack the implications further.

If the initiative to kill Jesus lay *solely* with the Jewish leaders and
the Romans that would mean God simply came in at the last minute
to snatch triumph from the jaws of defeat. Then the cross was *not*
his plan and purpose, the very reason why he sent his Son into the
world. That is totally unthinkable, for then Peter could not say it was
according to 'God's set purpose'.

If, however, it were the case that all the human agents (Judas,
Pilate, the chief priests and people) were non-responsible puppets,
then it makes no sense for Peter to call upon the people to *repent* for
what they have done. How can they repent for what they were
'forced' to do, as a puppet is 'forced' to sit at the bidding of the
strings pulled by the puppet master? They can't unless they made
the choices themselves. This would also mean that there was no sin
for which Jesus came to die, because in order to be guilty of sin one
has to be responsible for sinning. The Bible will not have that either.
Instead, we have the proper balanced picture: God was sovereignly
and providentially at work in the death of Jesus; human beings were
wicked in putting him to death *even* as they accomplished the Father's
will in doing so and God remains perfectly good.

Recognize the limits

It is at this juncture we tend to ask: 'How can this be so?' This brings us to our next point in facing up to our limitations and the restrictions of divine revelation. Remember the 'Melvin Method' of doing jigsaws – forcing pieces together and leaving other pieces out so we have no gaps? That is what in effect some do at this point.

There are those who so stress God's sovereignty that human beings are reduced to passive pieces on a cosmic chess board. It is reflected in the objection allegedly thrown at the great missionary, William Carey: 'If God wants the pagan converted, he will see to it without any help from us.' But the plain fact is, God has chosen certain *means* to achieve his designed ends, in this case that we explain the gospel to people in order for them to become Christians (we see this for example in Rom. 10:14–15, words which appear in the middle of one of the most predestinarian sections of the Bible, 'How, then, can they call on the one they have not believed in? And how can they believe in the one of whom they have not heard? And how can they hear without someone preaching to them?'). It might help to recognize the *non sequitur* involved if we think of a less controversial subject. One could say, 'If God wanted us to be clean, then he would ensure we are clean without any help from us.' But perhaps God does want us clean and that is why he has given us things like water, soap, showers and the like. We are to take action using the means God has provided.

On the other hand, there are those who, in wanting to preserve what they consider to be human freedom, maintain that God cannot know anything of future events until *after* we have acted. On this view God in effect ceases to be God as the Bible presents him, rather, it is human beings with considerable executive power who take central place. It is difficult to see on this view how God is little more than a caretaker God who comes along after us to clean up the mess and make the best of a bad job.[8]

How, then, does God's will and purpose relate to our wills and purposes in such a way that he overrules and we remain responsible agents? The short answer is: no one knows.[9] But then again we don't know the relation between so many things and we still manage to function. What is the relationship between my brain and my mind? The two are not the same. Is it that my mind is *within* the brain? Is it then that my thoughts are affected by the chemicals in my brain or is it that the functioning of my mind affects my brain? Is it the case that the brain is 'real' and my thoughts some kind of epiphenomenon? Or is there a duality of aspects – 'the brain story' and the 'mind story' – which are related in a complementary manner?[10] No one knows for certain. But the fact that we don't know the nature of this relationship doesn't stop us making decisions or ensuring we don't take drugs which will damage our brain and so affect our minds. So it is here with the relationship between God's rule and human responsibility. We can believe in *both* and act accordingly: 'To *man* belong the plans of the heart, *but* from the *Lord* comes the reply of the tongue' (Prov. 16:1). This theological position is given the term 'compatibilism', for it argues that God's sovereignty and human responsibility do not stand in contradiction to each other but are ultimately compatible, even if only in the mind of God.[11]

Hold the tension

After a thorough and extensive consideration of the biblical material and philosophical debate, D. A. Carson offers this sober conclusion:

> For us mortals there are no rational, logical solutions to the sovereignty–responsibility tension: it should be clear from the foregoing that neatly packaged harmonisations are impossible. But on the other hand, it is difficult to see why *logical* inconsistency is *necessitated,* especially in view of the many ambiguous parameters and numerous unknown quantities. The whole tension remains restless in our hands; but it is the restlessness of having a few randomly-selected pieces of a jigsaw puzzle when thousands more are needed to complete the design.[12]

C. H. Spurgeon was particularly gifted at reducing difficult things to a simple and memorable explanation. This is what he had to say

about the relation between God's sovereignty, upon which the
doctrine of providence is founded, and human choice:

> It is a difficult task to show the meeting place of the purpose of God
> and the free agency of man. One thing is quite clear; we are not to
> deny either of them, for they are both facts. It is a fact that God has
> purposed all things both great and little; neither will anything happen
> but according to his eternal purpose and decree. It is also a sure and
> certain fact that often times events hang upon the choice of men.
> Now how these two things can both be true I cannot tell you, neither
> probably after long debate could the wisest men in heaven tell you, not
> even with the consistence of cherubim and seraphim . . . They are two
> facts that run side by side, like parallel lines . . . Can you not believe
> them both? And is not the space between them a very convenient
> place to kneel in, adoring and worshipping him whom you cannot
> understand?[13]

Questions for reflection and discussion

1. Do you tend to underplay God's sovereignty or human
   responsibility? How does your approach need to become
   more biblically balanced?
2. 'He sovereignly rules over all while being God-in-relationship.'
   How does this compare with the view of God in the world
   around us?
3. Would you say that God takes risks? What difference does it
   make to us if he does or doesn't?
4. Consider how a well-balanced understanding of God's
   sovereignty and human responsibility will affect different
   aspects of your Christian life such as:
   • Evangelism
   • Prayer
   • Pursuing holiness
   • Making plans

Notes

1. I owe this illustration to D. A. Carson. Paul Helm makes a similar point: 'Christians do not reflect on these concepts in a purely abstract way and then try, in a wholly a priori fashion, to establish the concept's consistency. For we are constrained by the biblical witness as a set of fixed points, and then we must reflect upon the cogency or coherence of the several parts of that witness . . . it is not open to us to amend or modify that witness in any way in the interests of great comprehensibility. Faith seeks understanding, but the understanding gained must not be at the expense of the faith' (Paul Helm, 'The Augustinian-Calvinist View of Divine Foreknowledge', in James K. Beilby and Paul R. Eddy (eds.), *Divine Foreknowledge: Four Views* [InterVarsity Press, 2001], p. 164).

2. 'When we are faced with problems about the consistency of these concepts, it is tempting to modify one or both of them. But we must make every effort to avoid such a course of action. Scripture holds them together, it even speaks of them in the same breath, and so must we' (Helm, 'The Augustinian-Calvinist View', p. 167).

3. See, 'God or Chance?' in Donald M. MacKay, *The Clockwork Image* (Inter-Varsity Press, 1974), ch. 5.

4. P. T. Geach, *Providence and Evil* (Cambridge University Press, 1977), p. 34.

5. C. S. Lewis, *Prayer: Letters to Malcolm* (Fount, 1984), pp. 57–59.

6. One of the main objections to the 'risk free' view of providence is that for human beings to exercise genuine freedom, they must have the power to act contrary to God's purposes, indeed to be able to thwart them. This is known as the *libertarian* view of freedom: 'An agent is free with respect to a given action at a given time if at that time it is within the agent's power to perform the action and also in the agent's power to refrain from the action' (William Hasker, 'A Philosophical Perspective', in Pinnock *et al.*, *The Openness of God: A Biblical Challenge to the Traditional Understanding of God* [InterVarsity Press, 1994], pp. 136–137). This is to be distinguished from the *voluntarism* view of freedom (sometimes called 'freedom of inclination') as espoused, for example, by Jonathan Edwards, where we choose according to our nature, that is, we simply

do what we want to do: 'The ability to act according to his inclination and desires without being compelled to do otherwise by something or someone external to himself' (Sam Storms, *Chosen for Life* [Crossway, 2007], pp. 59–63). That the presupposition of the libertarian view is far from proven has been well demonstrated by Roger Nicole: 'Just about everyone agrees that in heaven there will be no more danger of apostasy. Does this mean that in glory men will be deprived of that freedom which constitutes the distinguishing character of humanity, the gift that stands so high that even the sovereign purpose of God must be viewed subordinate to it? Surely not. But if in glory perseverance is not inconsistent with freedom, why should it be thought incompatible on earth?' ('Some comments on Hebrews 6:4–6 and the Doctrine of the Perseverance of God with the Saints', in G. Hawthorne (ed.), *Current Issues in Biblical and Patristic Interpretation* [Eerdmans, 1975], p. 357, cited by D. A. Carson in *Divine Sovereignty and Human Responsibility Biblical Perspectives in Tension* [Marshal, Morgan and Scott, 1981], p. 208).

7. Donald Macleod, *A Faith to Live By* (Mentor-Christian Focus Publications, 1998).

8. There are those who are called 'free will theists' or upholders of the 'openness of God' who argue that God does not know what will happen in the future, but is only aware of the various possibilities of what *might* happen, e.g. Gregory A. Boyd, *God of the Possible: a Biblical Introduction to the Open View of God* (Baker Publishing, 2000) and John Sanders, *The God Who Risks: A Theology of Providence* (InterVarsity Press, 1998). This obviously has serious implications for how we conceive of prophecy in the Bible, such that it would not be possible for a prophecy to be made about Judas's betrayal, as this would violate his freedom, thus implying a certain inevitability about his actions and so relinquishing him of all responsibility. For a cogent presentation of the relation between compatibilism and prophecy see C. G. Tinker, 'God's Foreknowledge and Prophecy: A Case Study in Logical Indeterminism and Compatibilism', *Churchman* 118/1, 2006.

9. The reason for this is obvious: 'God's relation to the universe he has created and that he sustains and directs is a relation without parallel. It

is unique, incomparable, sui generis' (Helm, 'The Augustinian-Calvinist view', p. 167).

10. See Donald M. MacKay, in Melvin Tinker (ed.), *The Open Mind* (Inter-Varsity Press, 1988).

11. This viewpoint has been clearly presented by Paul Helm in *The Providence of God* (Inter-Varsity Press, 1993) and D. A. Carson, *How Long O Lord* (Inter-Varsity Press, [2]2006), ch. 11, 'The Mystery of Providence'.

12. D. A. Carson, *Divine Sovereignty and Human Responsibility: Biblical Perspectives in Tension* (Marshal, Morgan and Scott, 1981), p. 218. Similarly Macleod writes: 'There are many objections to this doctrine and most of them are philosophical rather than theological. Almost all of them are of this form: How do you reconcile election with this or that? How do you reconcile divine fore-ordination with human responsibility? How do you reconcile election and reprobation with the free offer of the Gospel? Any answer would also be philosophical. There is no theological (that is, revealed, biblical) solution to that dilemma. It is a problem of reconciling two equally important truths, but there is no biblical revelation of the solution to the problem' (*A Faith to Live By*, p. 50).

13. C. H. Spurgeon, Sermon 2303, 9 April 1893, *Metropolitan Tabernacle*, vol. 39, p. 169.

3. PROVIDENCE AND TIME (Psalm 90)

The picture painted so far of God's providence presupposes a certain understanding of the relationship between God and time. For example, in the previous chapter we referred to God as being 'outside time', the one who 'sees the end from the beginning'. But how might this be conceived and what would it entail? You would not be surprised to find that this subject has generated endless philosophical debate which we are not able to fully enter into here.[1] Instead, we shall take a look at the 'classic' position which this book follows, but by beginning with a consideration of how we encounter and envisage time in our Western postmodern culture. Our starting point will therefore be a more practical one and in due course we shall think through some of the implications our view of providence has on how we might conduct our lives in the light of eternity.

All the time in the world?

'What then *is* time? If no one asks me, I know; if I want to explain
it to a questioner, I do not know.'[2] So writes the great Augustine
of Hippo. In more recent times the physicist, Lee Smolin has said,
'I have been studying the question of what time is for much of my
adult life. But I must admit . . . that I am no closer to an answer now
than I was then. Indeed, even after all this study; I do not think we
can answer even the simple question: "What sort of thing is time?"'[3]
It has to be admitted that thinking about time can cause us major
headaches; how much more will that be the case when we consider
the relationship between time and eternity! Leaving aside the philosophical issues for a moment,[4] let us think through how most of us
envisage time and so order life's priorities.

Meet Mr Modern: he is digitalized, diarized and highly organized.
Time means money. Mr Modern wastes no time, he refuses to
surrender to the trivial at the expense of the significant, and the
important is never to be sacrificed on the altar of the urgent.
Mr Modern lives life in the fast lane, lunch is for wimps, time means
money; more money to spend on more leisure, but there seems so
little time for leisure. Mr Modern is important, indispensable, and
can be contacted anywhere at any time, courtesy of his smartphone.
A moment of quiet intrudes into Mr Modern's precious time as his
mind wanders for a moment and settles on those two little figures
he left lying in bed at home. How old were they now? Five and six,
or was it eight and nine? Goodness, how time flies! He must, simply
must, spend more time with them. Yes, that's what he will do next
year – time permitting, of course.

Although he does not know it, Mr Modern is a victim of a new
tyranny, the tyranny of time. It was the novelist Henry Fielding who
was the first to write that 'time is money'. Charles Baudelaire spoke
of the mechanical clock as 'the sinister god'. This is the modern
view of time. Time is a *commodity* to be bought and sold. Time is an
opportunity to be active, in business and in leisure, and the more that
can be crammed into it the better. And so we have developed some

rather interesting sayings; we 'buy time', 'maximize time' and even make sure that we have 'quality time'.[5] Throughout at the back of our mind is the thought that what I can't do today, I can put off until tomorrow, while never considering that there may be no tomorrow. Part of this new attitude towards time is that the future is often taken for granted. In the words of the musical *Fame,* people behave as if they are going to live for ever.

Although we dream of having more leisure and so fill our lives with labour-saving devices to achieve this, the pace somehow never seems to slacken. As we try to fit as much as possible into the day and squeeze the last drop of life out of each hour, we seem to suffer for it. Time, it appears, can seriously damage our health, not to mention our work, families and even our spiritual life. After all, who has time for God? Of course, it is not time *per se* but our attitude towards it that causes such modern phenomena as burnout and breakdowns.

The view of time as a commodity is relatively recent, dating from the industrial revolution and the invention of accurate timepieces in the eighteenth century. With the rise of industry came the idea of *time* management. Henry Ford said of his ideal worker, 'He must have every second necessary, but not a single unnecessary second.'[6]

A modern problem

Part of our modern time-drivenness is that many have lost any sense that our lives constitute a story, a purposeful narrative, that what matters is what we make of our lives, having them being given shape and direction by who we are and what we do. For many today life tends to be fragmented, with little sense of the past and little concern for the future. One of the dominant features of postmodernism is the lack of what is called a 'meta-narrative', an overall, overarching story which gives meaning to what we do and who we are. The result is that we live for the moment, the instant, filling our lives with activities as an alcoholic fills his stomach with drink. The existentialist philosopher, Martin Heidegger, called this presumption in the way we view the present as 'the proudly Exclusive Now' or indeed, as 'the strutting point'.

The havoc to family life caused by this view of time has been well captured by the song, 'The Cat's in the Cradle'. The real tragedy of this song resides in the life of the man who recorded it, Harry Chapin. His wife actually wrote the lyrics and asked him one day when he was going to slow down his frantic pace of life and give some time to his children. His answer was: 'At the end of this busy summer, I'll take some time to be with them.' That summer, Harry Chapin was killed in a car accident.

Back to the Bible

How we view time has far-reaching practical consequences, for good or ill, for our lives as individuals, a society and a church.

How, then, according to the Scriptures, should we think of time and have our lives shaped accordingly? Psalm 90 provides a useful starting point to answer such questions.

The first thing we are to ponder is that God is timeless. On the face of it that appears to be what the psalmist is asserting: 'Before the mountains were born or you brought forth the earth and the world, from everlasting to everlasting you are God' (Ps. 90:2). This view of God's relation to time has been proposed by such thinkers as Boethius,[7] Thomas Aquinas,[8] Calvin[9] and Schleiermacher.[10]

Here is Boethius:[11]

> It is the common judgement, then, of all creatures that live by reason that God is eternal. So let us consider the nature of eternity, for this will make clear to us both the nature of God and his manner of knowing. *Eternity, then, is the complete, simultaneous and perfect possession of everlasting life* . . . And if human and divine present may be compared, just as you see certain things in this your present time, so God sees all things in His eternal present.[12]

Aquinas says something similar, 'God's knowledge, like his existence, is measured by eternity, which in one and the same instant encompasses all time; so his gaze is eternally focused on everything in time as on something present . . . What happens in time is known by us in time, moment by moment, but by God in an eternal moment, above time.'[13]

Thus for God 'our time' takes on a different 'configuration' from his perspective, 'For a thousand years in your sight are like a day that has just gone by' (Ps. 90:4). The apostle Peter echoes the same thought, 'With the Lord a day is like a thousand years, and a thousand years are like a day' (2 Pet. 3:8). Time can only be measured in an arena where change takes place. Our bodies grow old, our cars wear out, rivers flow to the sea and so on. But supposing we lived in a world which was changeless. What if our eyes could not only move left and right, but backwards and forwards in *time* so that we could perceive the horizons of history as well as the horizons of our globe? In short, what if we lived in eternity? What would our time look like from *that* perspective? Then such a being would see everything within 'one eternal moment' and would plan with 'all in view', the 'end from the beginning'. Nothing would take him by surprise, nothing would be left to chance; like the mind of an author conceiving a book, all the characters and their histories appear at once, their past, present and future are seen together in the eternal Now.[14] Why should this not be the case with God and the world?[15]

To enable us to grasp how we might begin to conceive this relationship between a timeless God and creatures like ourselves who are bound by time, C. S. Lewis suggests the following: 'If you picture Time as a straight line along which we have to travel, then you must picture God as the whole page on which the line is drawn. We come to the parts of the line one by one: we have to leave A behind before we get to B, and we cannot reach C until we leave B behind. God, from above or outside or all round, contains the whole line, and sees all.'[16]

All of this, of course, stands in such stark contrast to us who are bound by time. We grow old, change our plans, and diminish in our intellectual, physical and spiritual powers. Our youthfulness eventually gives way to decrepitude if we live long enough. In short, we are mortal: 'You sweep men away in the sleep of death; they are like the new grass of the morning – though in the morning it springs up new, by evening it is dry and withered' (Ps. 90:5). For human beings, time is a gift allotted by the everlasting God: 'The length of our days is seventy years – or eighty, if we have the strength' (Ps. 90:10).[17]

A change of view

Let us now tease out some of the implications of this view of the timeless God, the Creator of all (including time) and our attitude towards time which comes under his providential rule.

First, instead of thinking of time as a commodity which we possess, 'Don't take up *my* time', we should see it as a gracious gift which is on loan. It is first and foremost *God's* time.[18] This will mean, as Paul says in Ephesians 5:16, the Christian will seek to redeem the time, 'making the most of every opportunity'. He or she will desire to be a careful steward of time as we should with every other aspect of God's creation. Here is Paul's exposition of this principle:

> Be very careful, then, how you live – not as unwise but wise, making the most of every opportunity [lit. redeeming the time], because the days are evil. Therefore do not be foolish, but understand what the Lord's will is. Do not get drunk on wine, which leads to debauchery. Instead, be filled with the Spirit. Speak to one another with psalms, hymns and spiritual songs. Sing and make music in your heart to the Lord, always giving thanks to God the Father for everything, in the name of our Lord Jesus Christ (Eph. 5:15–20).

In other words, fools squander this gift in directionless and selfish waste, like getting drunk. A number of years ago the writer and broadcaster Clive James conducted an interview with the actor

Mel Gibson who made this very point. Gibson, looking back on his 'hell-raising' younger days when he would drink heavily and do the most outrageous things, lamented that nothing is as wasteful as getting drunk.

Likewise, the apostle Paul earlier on in Ephesians gives a list of things which characterize a waste of time and so a wasted life: fornicating, lying, stealing, backbiting, dirty story-telling, greed (4:17 – 5:4). These contribute nothing constructive, instead they demean others and corrupt ourselves; and at the end of their lives that is the 'story' those who do such things will have written and which will be presented to God to judge. In contrast, Paul calls Christians to 'be filled with the Spirit' and the writer of Psalm 90 asks of God to 'teach us to number our days aright, that we may gain a heart of wisdom' (v. 12).

This means that horizontally in our relationships with each other, we should seek to build each other up with the beautiful truths of God – singing psalms, spiritual songs – ministering to one another (Eph. 5:19–20). That is a productive use of time, something for which we were originally created.

Vertically, we are to give thanks to God, which ultimately is what Christian believers will be doing in eternity, immersed in heart-felt, joyful, loving praise to so glorious a Saviour. Whatever we do 'in word or deed' we are to 'do it all in the name of the Lord Jesus, giving thanks to God the Father through him' (Col. 3:17).

It also means we should embrace the notion of 'rest'. Being harried and hurried, fretting and fussing have become everyday features of modern Western life and Christians can easily be caught up in these as much as anyone else. But to believe that God is in control over all, reigning providentially and not subject to the vagaries of space and time while still active in space and time, allows the Christian to rest in the Lord. This is where the biblical notion of 'Sabbath' comes into play. The climax to God's creative activity in Genesis 1 and 2 is God 'resting', which is the verb found in Genesis 2:2, *šābat*, from which we get our word 'Sabbath', a term which has the basic meaning of 'ceasing'. When we use the word 'rest' we associate it with inactivity, but here it has associations of the completion of a certain activity and the entering into a new state of affairs (which is described by a different set of words, the verb *nûaḥ* and noun *měnûḥâ*, in Exod. 20:11: entering into a position of stability and security).[19] Thus, with the whole cosmos as God's temple and acting as 'sacred space', God is ruling for his glory and his people's wellbeing. A visible sign and expression that God's followers really do believe this will be to cease from their normal activities on what Christians in the early church came to call the 'Lord's Day' (cf. Acts 20:7; 1 Cor. 16:2; Rev. 1:10). John H. Walton puts the matter this way:

> When we 'rest' on the Sabbath, we recognise him [God] as the author of
> order and the one who brings rest (stability) to our lives in the world. We
> take our hands off the controls of our lives and acknowledge him as the
> one who is in control. Most importantly this calls on us to step back
> from our workaday world, those means by which we try to provide for
> ourselves and gain control of our circumstances. Sabbath is for
> recognising that it is God who provides for us and who is master of our
> lives and our world . . . It is the way that we recognise that God is on the
> throne, that this world is his world, that our time is God's gift to us.[20]

One final practical and eminently pastoral implication of our view of providence and time is the relief of anxiety about the future. In his book, *Respectable Sins*,[21] Jerry Bridges pinpoints anxiety as a 'respectable sin' we too easily come to terms with. He writes, 'Anxiety is a sin . . . because it is a lack of acceptance of God's providence in our lives. God's providence may be simply defined as God's orchestrating all circumstances and events in his universe for His glory and the good of His people.'[22] He then recounts some wise words on the subject offered by John Newton in a letter to a friend:

> [One of the marks of Christian maturity which a believer should seek is]
> an acquiescence in the Lord's will founded in a persuasion of his
> wisdom, holiness, sovereignty and goodness . . . So far as we attain this,

we are secure from disappointment. Our own limited views, and short-sighted purposes and desires, may be, and will be, often over-ruled; but then our main and leading desire, that the will of the Lord may be done, must be accomplished. How highly does it become us, both as creatures and as sinners, to submit to the appointments of our maker! And how necessary is it to our peace! This great attainment is too often unthought of, and over-looked; we are prone to fix our attention upon the second causes and immediate instruments of events; forgetting that whatever befalls us is according to his purpose, and therefore must be right and seasonable in itself, and shall in the issue be productive of good. From hence arise impatience, resentment, and secret repinings (i.e., complaining), which are not only sinful, but tormenting; whereas, if all things are in his hand, if the very hairs of our head are numbered; if every event, great and small, is under the direction of his providence and purpose; and if he has a wise, holy and gracious end in view, to which everything that happens is subordinate and subservient; then we have nothing to do, but with patience and humility follow as he leads, and cheerfully to expect a happy issue . . . How happy are they who can resign all to him, see his hand in every dispensation, and believe that he chooses better for them than they possibly could for themselves.[23]

Before the God of time who dwells in timeless eternity, may our prayer be that of the psalmist, 'Teach us to number our days aright, that we may gain a heart of wisdom.'

Questions for reflection and discussion

1. How do those around you treat their time?
2. In what ways does the way you treat time influence your relationship with God?
3. Make a list of all the ways that we are affected by time (e.g. we get old). Then beside that make a list of all the implications of God not being affected by time (e.g. he never ages).

4. Look through Ephesians 5:15–20 and consider what changes you might make to your life to 'redeem the time'.

5. How might it affect the life of your church family if you treat your time as a gift from God?

Notes

1. For a helpful presentation of the four major views of God's relationship with time see Gregory E. Ganssle (ed.), *God and Time* (InterVarsity Press, 2001).

2. Augustine, *Confessions*, Ch. XI, Section XIV.

3. Lee Smolin, 'What is time?', in J. Brockman and K. Matson (eds.), *How Things Are* (Wiedenfield and Nicholson, 1995).

4. For an excellent introduction to this topic see Stephen Bishop, 'God, Time and Eternity', *Quodlibet Journal* 6/1, January – March 2004. ISSN: 1526-6575.

5. See Os Guinness, *Prophetic Untimeliness – A Challenge to the Idol of Relevance* (Baker Books, 2003), pp. 27–45, for a penetrating critique of the modern concept of time from a biblical viewpoint.

6. Quoted in Guinness, *Prophetic Untimeliness*.

7. Boethius, *Consolation of Philosophy*, Bk 5, tr. E. V. Watts (Penguin Classics, 1969).

8. Thomas Aquinas, *Summa Theologica, A Concise Translation*, ed. Timothy McDermott (London: Methuen, 1991).

9. John Calvin, *Institutes*, III.21.5, ed. John T. McNeill (Westminster, 1960).

10. F. Schleiermacher, *The Christian Faith* (T. & T. Clark, 1999), §52–53. For a more recent presentation of this position see Paul Helm, *The Eternal God: A Study of God Without Time* (Clarendon Press, 1988).

11. It is quite clear that Boethius was a major influence on the thinking of C. S. Lewis in this area, e.g. 'Time and Beyond Time' in *Mere Christianity* (Fount, 1978), Bk 4, ch. 3.

12. *Consolation*, 5.6.

13. *Summa Theologica*, 14.13.

14. This analogy has been developed to great effect by Dorothy L. Sayers in her book, *The Mind of the Maker* (Mowbray, 1994).

15. John Frame offers a cautionary warning about how we conceive God's relation to time in terms of atemporality: 'I have argued that God's transcendence is not his being outside or beyond history, but rather his being Lord and King, in control of all things and speaking with authority over all things. So God's special relation to time, whether temporal or atemporal, should not be defined first in terms of temporality, but in terms of lordship' ('Lord of Time', in John Frame, *The Doctrine of God* [P. & R. Publishing, 2002], p. 557).

16. Lewis, *Mere Christianity*, p. 144.

17. Terrence Tiessen's summary of God's relation to time is one we might wish to adopt: 'God's relationship to time and, hence, the nature of eternity is mysterious. However, we can affirm that God transcends our time (as he does our space), in the sense that he is not limited by it as we are. He is present in all time (and space) but is not restricted by it. We can also affirm that God is nevertheless able to act in time, as he does in space, and to establish and discern the time relationship of different events' (*Providence and Prayer. How does God work in the world?* [InterVarsity Press, 2000], p. 331).

18. 'I believe that there are some assertions we can make about God and time that are important to our understanding of providence. For starters, our time is God's gift to us, and we do better to think of our time being within God's "time" than of him being in ours' (Tiessen, *Providence and Prayer,* p. 321).

19. See John H. Walton, *The Lost World of Genesis One* (InterVarsity Press, 2009), pp. 72–77.

20. Walton, *Lost World,* p. 147, also G. K. Beale, *The Temple and the Church's Mission: A Biblical Theology of the Dwelling Place of God* (Apollos, 2004), p. 62: 'God's rest both at the conclusion of creation in Genesis 1 – 2 and later in Israel's temple indicates not mere inactivity but that he had demonstrated his sovereignty over the forces of chaos (e.g., the enemies of Israel) and now has assumed a position of kingly rest revealing his sovereign power.'

21. Jerry Bridges, *Respectable Sins* (NavPress, 2007).
22. *Respectable Sins,* p. 64.
23. *Respectable Sins,* p. 66.

4. PROVIDENCE IN ACTION (Joseph)

Sir Winston Churchill was a man who was consumed by an extraordinary sense of providence and personal destiny. Aware of this he went on to lead a nation, championing the cause of freedom against overwhelming odds. On the night of 10th May 1940, Churchill was invited by King George VI to form a government to take on the forces of Nazi tyranny which threatened the entire free world. Later Churchill recounted, 'I felt as if I were walking with destiny and that all my past life had been but a preparation for this hour and this trial.'

Adolf Hitler also believed in destiny – *Schicksal*. In 1937 he said, 'When I look back upon the five years that lie behind, I can say that this was not the work of human hands alone.' But as time progressed we see a contradiction developing in Hitler. On the one hand he began to see himself as something bigger than fate, being able to control it, but when he wanted to avoid making a decision, he simply called on his *Vorsehung*, his 'Providence' (passive, cold and dark), then (rather conveniently some might add) it was all a matter of 'whatever will be will be'.

I would suspect that today more people would side with Hitler than with Churchill at this point. Not that they would subscribe to his racist fantasies, but they would nonetheless go through life on the basis that there is nothing but blind, impersonal fate at work.

Churchill's views, however, were much nearer to those of the Bible, namely, that there is a personal wholly good Being who is actively at work in and through all things in a purposeful way. As the term implies, to speak of providence is, amongst other things, making the claim that it is God who *provides*. As such it is not just the stuff of academic debate, it is down-to-earth and deeply practical and, as we shall see, immensely reassuring.

There is one story in the Bible which perhaps above all others illustrates God's remarkable providence, with God working not only behind the scenes but within every scene, often unobserved (except to the eye of faith) and in ways we could not even begin to imagine. It is the story of Joseph. This is such a well-known and well-loved story that even a musical by Andrew Lloyd Webber has been made out of it. It begins in Genesis 37 with Joseph just seventeen years old, whose job it was to tend his father's flock. He is quite good looking too by all accounts and what is more he is a 'Daddy's boy':

> Now Israel loved Joseph more than any of his other sons, because he
> had been born to him in his old age; and he made a richly
> ornamented robe for him. When his brothers saw that their father loved
> him more than any of them, they hated him and could not speak a kind
> word to him (vv. 3–4).

Therefore, at the beginning of the story we have paternal favouritism at work. When this is combined with youthful impudence, we have a heady mix which has all the makings of a major family drama as Joseph tells his eleven brothers that he had a dream which portrayed them bowing down in subservience to him:

> Joseph had a dream, and when he told it to his brothers, they hated him
> all the more. He said to them, 'Listen to this dream I had: We were

binding sheaves of grain out in the field when suddenly my sheaf rose and stood upright, while your sheaves gathered around mine and bowed down to it.' His brothers said to him, 'Do you intend to reign over us? Will you actually rule us?' And they hated him all the more because of his dream and what he had said (Gen. 37:5–8).

That is decidedly not the best way to win friends and influence people! Fuelled by jealousy, his brothers hatch a plot to kill him. This is later modified to selling him into slavery as a group of Ishmaelite merchants just 'happen' to turn up on the scene (37:25).

Eventually Joseph finds himself in the household of a rich Egyptian nobleman called Potiphar (Gen. 39). After some years he is placed in overall charge of all his property, which is a remarkable feat for an outsider. Everything looks like it is turning out rosy, that is, until the mistress of the house tries to seduce him. When Joseph spurns her advances, in a fit of jealous rage she lies through her teeth, claiming that Joseph had tried to rape her. In a terrible twist of injustice Joseph finds himself in prison where his dream-interpreting gifts are used to predict the future of two fellow prisoners: the restoration of Pharaoh's cupbearer and the death of his baker. Promising to put in a good word for him when he is released, the cupbearer promptly forgets all about him, and Joseph is left behind to rot. But there is then a further twist in the drama as Pharaoh himself is plagued by a recurring bad dream. Believing it is no accident but a portent of the gods, he wants the dream interpreted. No one in the court can do it. It is then that the cupbearer remembers Joseph, who becomes the man of the moment. He is brought before the king and God gives him the power to interpret what the dream means – that after seven years of great harvests there will be seven years of famine. What is more, Joseph offers some prudent advice concerning steps which might be taken to alleviate the effects of the famine. Pharaoh is suitably impressed, and Joseph is in effect made prime minister (Gen. 41).

It is during the years of famine that Joseph's brothers approach him for help, not realizing who he is (Gen. 42). In one of the most heart-rending reconciliation scenes ever written, Joseph and his family are restored (Gen. 45). Their father, who had all this time believed Joseph to be dead, eventually makes his way to the palace. Not only are they saved from the famine, but so is most of the country and the surrounding area, and the whole family settle for a prosperous life in Egypt.

It is important to realize that this is not a story of the 'they all lived happily ever after' variety. It has to be considered in its wider context of God's plan of salvation for the world. God had promised Abraham back in Genesis 12 that through *his* descendants (and one in particular) the whole earth would be blessed. He was referring to how he would bring about the world's rescue from sin and judgment.[1] Later, in Genesis 15, God tells Abraham that for a while some of his immediate descendants would live in a foreign land and be enslaved for four hundred years before God would restore them to the land of promise (i.e. they would be captive in Egypt before Moses set them free, Gen. 15:13–14). But the crucial question is this: what guarantee is there that this would happen? Was it possible, for example, that someone might come along and upset God's plans so that either Abraham's offspring would not find themselves in Egypt or once there, remain there? In other words, does God ever take risks?

The understanding of providence which we have been considering gives the answer to that question as an indefatigable 'no'. God's saving purposes in the world are 'risk free'. In order to help us understand a little more clearly what this entails, we shall look at two parts of the Joseph story, starting at the end and then moving to nearer the beginning.

The principle of providence (Gen. 50:19–21)

Here is the situation: with their father Jacob dead, the brothers are terrified that Joseph will use the opportunity to exact revenge for the shabby way they had treated him, and so they appear to make up a message which they claim to be the last wish of their father:

So they sent word to Joseph saying, 'Your father left these instructions
before he died: "This is what you are to say to Joseph: I ask you to
forgive your brothers the sins and the wrongs they have committed in
treating you badly." Now please forgive the sins of the servants of the
God of your father' (Gen. 50:16–17).

But Joseph's character is not like theirs, he sees things differently
and more generously: 'Joseph said to them, "Don't be afraid. Am I
in the place of God? You intended to harm me, but God intended
it for good to accomplish what is now being done, the saving of
many lives. So then, don't be afraid, I will provide for you and your
children"' (v. 19).

D. A. Carson offers some perceptive reflections on this incident
by noting what Joseph does *not* say:

> He does not say that during a momentary lapse on God's part, Joseph's
> brothers sold him into slavery, but that God, being a superb chess player,
> turned the game around and in due course made Joseph prime minister
> of Egypt. Still less does he say that God's intention had been to send
> Joseph in a well-appointed chariot, but unfortunately Joseph's brothers
> rather mucked up the divine plan, forcing God to respond with clever
> counter moves to bring about his own good purposes. Rather, *in the one
> event*, the selling of Joseph into slavery, there were two parties, and two
> quite different intentions. On the one hand, Joseph's brothers acted, and
> their intentions were evil; on the other, God acted, and his intentions
> were good. Both acted to bring about this event, but while the evil in it
> must be traced back to the brothers and no further, the good must be
> traced back to God.[2]

Theologically, this paradox is known as 'double agency'. Here the
meaning and purpose of the primary agent (in this case God) is to
be found in the secondary agents' (the brothers') action, but there
is no guarantee that they are meaning or intending the same thing.
It was the philosopher Austin Farrer who proposed this idea:
'Everything that is done in this world by intelligent creatures is done

with two meanings: the meaning of the creature acting, the meaning of the Creator in founding or supporting that action. Subjectively considered, there are two doings; physically there is but one event.'[3] This does not mean that God was 'forcing' the brothers to behave in the way they did, which was wicked (otherwise God would be the author of evil); they freely chose this course of action, with malicious intentions. Nonetheless, through such human choices God achieved his primary and specific intention of establishing Joseph in a place of responsibility in order to bring blessing upon the wider world at that time and, as we shall see, the whole world at a later point in time through one of his descendants, thus fulfilling God's promise to Abraham in Genesis 12:

> 'I will make you into a great nation,
>   and I will bless you;
> I will make your name great,
>   and you will be a blessing.
> I will bless those who bless you,
>   and whoever curses you I will curse;
> and all peoples on earth
>   will be blessed through you' (vv. 2–3).

What does this tell us about providence?

First of all it reveals that providence is *personal*: '*God* intended.' He is the one overseeing and superintending our lives. He doesn't take an occasional glance to see what is going on and at odd times intervene; he is there at every moment, before, during and after whatever is happening and is intimately and personally involved. We are meant to find that truth immensely reassuring.

Secondly, providence is *purposeful*: 'God intended it *for good*.' The things that happened to Joseph were not accidental, lacking meaning and significance, they were all part of God's design to bring about good ends. There were several goods which we, the reader, can discern. It cannot be denied that it was good for Joseph that he secured such an influential position, second only to Pharaoh. God intended that to happen. It was good for the brothers and Jacob, Joseph's father, not only in reforming their character but also in saving their lives from starvation. God by his providence provides for them through Joseph. It was also good for Egypt and the surrounding nations because God had brought Joseph with his gifts and wisdom at this point in time to Egypt with the result that through his prudent policy many lives were saved.

However, these events were also to produce goods well beyond the lifetime of the characters involved in the drama. This was the means whereby God preserved the twelve sons of Jacob from which were to come the twelve tribes of Israel, from which in turn was to come Jesus Christ the Saviour of the world:

> You are a lion's cub, O Judah;
>> you return from the prey, my son.
> Like a lion he crouches and lies down,
>> like a lioness – who dares to rouse him?
> The sceptre will not depart from Judah,
>> nor the ruler's staff from between his feet,
> until he to whom it belongs shall come
>> and the obedience of the nations shall be his (Gen. 49:9–10).

God in his infinite wisdom and omnipotence is able not just to 'kill two birds with one stone', but millions, for he is able to hold all events, all human decisions, all options and know all actual and possible outcomes in his mind in an eternal moment, so ensuring that his will is done for our good and his glory.

Thirdly, providence is *all embracing*. God was not just working in the life of Joseph, although he is the central character in this drama at this point in the story of redemption, he is at work in *everyone's* life. He is actively weaving the whole interconnecting web which is made up of every thought, decision and action. In other words, there aren't any 'no go' areas in his universe which God allows to be, as it were, free-floating. The fact is that every single detail of our life, from our genetic composition to whom we happen to meet on the way to the shops, is, to a greater or lesser degree, significant in shaping not only who we are but what we will become. Think of all the details that have gone into the make up of this story which if they had been even slightly different at any point would have produced a totally different story with a different ending: the buying of the ornate coat, the relating of the dream, the oafishness of the brothers, the kindness of one of them, their jealousy, all of which led to the selling of Joseph into slavery.

Consider the following: had the Ishmaelite merchants not come along when they did, or had not been a group involved in the slave trade, this would have meant no Joseph in slavery in Egypt. Or then again, if there had been no Potiphar, this would entail no position of responsibility, no Potiphar's wife, no prison sentence, which in turn would have meant no meeting Pharaoh's cupbearer, no meeting Pharaoh, no premiership, no saving people from famine, no twelve tribes of Israel, no fulfilling of God's promises to Abraham, no Jesus Christ, no Saviour of the world and no Christianity. This illustrates how *everything* is interconnected to everything else; there is, if you like, a divine-human 'butterfly effect' going on and so God has to be at work in *every* link in the chain, or to change the imagery slightly, every strand in the complex web, to ensure that his good, eternal purposes are carried out.

Fourthly, providence involves *human responsibility*. God does not override our choices; he knows them, uses them and holds us accountable for them. The brothers still did evil; they can't get off the hook by rolling their eyes in a pious fashion claiming they were simply fulfilling God's plans for *they* had no such intention. What is more, Joseph was only used by God as he developed in character. Presumably, once he arrived in Egypt he had to learn the language and develop the accounting and administrative skills expected of the top steward. He would have made numerous decisions as prime minister, he wasn't a puppet. God *uses* our choices, he does not *abuse* them.

All of this is borne out in the account of Joseph in the household of Potiphar and in prison.

The evidence of providence (Gen. 39)

If you were Joseph at what point would you have said: 'Is God really with me?' Wouldn't you take it as a sign of God's blessing that you had landed a pretty good job with Potiphar? On the face of it that is what the narrator of our story appears to be saying in verse 2: 'The LORD was with Joseph and he prospered, and he lived in the house of his Egyptian master.' So is it right as some Christians today would claim, that God wants us to be prosperous, having a healthy family, plenty of money, a great job and an all-round good life and in these we see the presence of God in our lives? One might be tempted to think such a thing if it were not for the end of the episode in verses 20–21, 'But while Joseph was in there in prison, the LORD was with him.' This is almost the same phraseology as at the beginning of the chapter and so forms the literary envelope (*inclusio*) of this particular episode. I don't know about you, but I would have been tempted to have thought, 'Yes, God was with me in the palace, but he abandoned me in the prison.' No, the Lord was with Joseph in *both* places. He is not just the God of the good times but of the hard times as well. This means that if we are finding things especially difficult at the moment we are not to take that as a sign of God abandoning us, any more than Joseph took his jail sentence as a sign of God abandoning him. God was there using that experience as well.

What is more, the narrator's comment that the Lord was with Joseph in Potiphar's house refers not only to his good position, but his enabling to make the right moral stand in the face of temptation:

> Joseph found favour in his eyes and became his attendant. Potiphar put him in charge of his household, and he entrusted to his care everything he owned. From the time he put him in charge of his household and of all that he owned, the LORD blessed the household of the Egyptian because of Joseph. The blessing of the LORD was on everything Potiphar had, both in the house and in the field. So he left in Joseph's care

everything he had; with Joseph in charge, he did not concern himself with anything except the food he ate.

Now Joseph was well-built and handsome, and after a while his master's wife took notice of Joseph and said, 'Come to bed with me!' But he refused. 'With me in charge,' he told her, 'my master does not concern himself with anything in the house; everything he owns he has entrusted to my care. No one is greater in this house than I am. My master has withheld nothing from me except you, because you are his wife. How then could I do such a wicked thing and sin against God?' And though she spoke to Joseph day after day, he refused to go to bed with her or even be with her (Gen: 39:4–10).

Can you even begin to imagine how strong the pull must have been to give in to that kind of temptation? Not only is there the obvious hormonal charge of a young man, which must have been particularly vexing, but here is a youth far from home, no family, in an alien land and so no-one to whom he had to give an account. He was in a position where, to be frank, he could have managed to get away with an illicit affair had he so wished. What is striking is what motivated him in his chastity (which forms a stark and deliberate contrast to his brother Judah in the previous chapter), namely, his fear of offending God and betraying the trust of his master. As Potiphar's wife battered on the door of his life, night after lonely night, what but God's grace could enable him to make such a stand? Yes, the Lord was with Joseph all right!

We may ask: What lessons might Joseph have learnt? He must have learnt something, for it seems that the cocksure young man of chapter 37 with his great dreams of grandeur has given way to a very different and a more caring man in chapter 50. When did that character formation begin? No doubt on his long journey to Egypt hand-bound as a slave. It is highly likely that he engaged in intense contemplation and prayer on those lonely nights in Potiphar's house. How might we think he felt at the glimmer of hope when the cupbearer was released and said, 'Yes I won't forget you, I will put in a good word', and promptly didn't? In all probability he felt devastated. And yet at each step of the way God was using such circumstances to make Joseph into the man he wanted him to become in order to fulfil the plans he designed. Even Churchill had his 'wilderness years' when he was considered to be a political 'has been', but that too was used to make him into the great leader he was to become. If times are good, bless God, if times are hard, God can still be blessed and trusted.

It is also worth noting the timescale involved. Such a change did not take place by the following Tuesday! The amount of time which passed between the Potiphar's wife episode and reconciliation with his brothers was around twenty years. God's timescale is not necessarily the same as ours. Providence both requires patience and is a means of producing it.

This, however, raises a further question: How did Joseph reach the conclusion, 'God intended it for good'? It certainly wasn't simply a matter of reading it off from the circumstances. How can one conclude that God is achieving a good purpose by being sold into slavery? How can one even begin to take comfort from being thrown out of the house, unjustly being accused of attempted rape when all you tried to do was to keep God's law in not committing adultery, and that this was 'for the good of many'? It can't be done. In fact the events could have been read in lots of different ways; that God *wasn't* in control, that the devil was in charge and that the wicked do seem to prevail and so on. The only apparent reason why Joseph could believe what he did, which led him to make this profound statement, was because God had revealed it, a revelation confirmed by hindsight in experience. Joseph would have known something of God. His father was Jacob after all, who had had plenty of revelations of God. He too would have had stories passed on to him by his father Isaac who in turn would have had stories related to him by Abraham.[4] This means he would have known of God's promises and his work in the lives of his forefathers. No doubt he would have reflected long and hard on those things. In other words, he would have been walking by faith, not by sight, relying on God being as good as his word and the belief

that God intends good for his chosen people in spite of what others
might intend.

Towards the end of his life as Joseph looks back he can see part
of the picture of what God has achieved. But it is only *part* of the
picture. He hadn't the slightest inkling of the overwhelming goods
which God was going to bring about in the future; especially that
eventually another shepherd boy would be born, called David, a
shepherd King, and that from him *the* Shepherd King would be born,
Jesus of Nazareth. This one was also to suffer a grotesque act of
injustice and betrayal resulting in imprisonment and beatings, only
to be finally impaled on a cross. But God also intended this for good
and 'the saving of many lives'.

We may not be a Joseph but Christians are in God's good purposes
nonetheless, so even though in the midst of circumstances we may
not be able to discern God's *immediate* purposes, we can believe they
are not accidents. There may be times in the future when, like Joseph,
we can look back and say, 'Now I see it, I understand at least in part
what God was doing'. But there will be many times when we will
simply have to say 'I don't know, but God does and I will trust in
him anyway'.

Here is part of a parable told by Professor Basil Mitchell which
illustrates the relationship between having some understanding, lack
of complete understanding and trust:

> In time of war in an occupied country, a member of the resistance one
> night meets a stranger who deeply impresses him. They spend that night
> together in conversation. The stranger tells the partisan that he himself
> is on the side of the resistance – indeed that he is in command of it, and
> urges the partisan to have faith in him no matter what happens. The
> partisan is utterly convinced at that meeting of the stranger's sincerity
> and constancy and undertakes to trust him.
>
> They never meet in conditions of intimacy again. But sometimes the
> stranger is seen helping members of the resistance, and the partisan is
> grateful and says to his friends, 'He is on our side.' Sometimes he is seen
> in the uniform of the police handing over patriots to the occupying

power. On these occasions his friends murmur against him: but the partisan still says, 'He is on our side.' He still believes that, in spite of appearances, the stranger did not deceive him. Sometimes he asks the stranger for help and receives it. He is thankful. Sometimes he asks and does not receive it. Then he says, 'The stranger knows best.'[5]

For us, however, God is not a stranger; he has revealed himself as a friend in the face of Jesus Christ. We therefore return full circle to that key thematic text of Romans 8:28, 'In all things God works for the good for those who love him, who are called according to his purpose.'

Questions for reflection and discussion

1. 'You intended to harm me, but God intended it for good.' Are there any parts of your life where there were human intentions for good or bad, but now you can see God's greater, providential purposes?
2. How should we face situations where we struggle to see the purpose of God, even a long time afterwards?
3. What does the incident of Joseph and Potiphar's wife teach about God's providence in the face of temptation?
4. Are there times when you wonder whether God is with you? What difference does the story of Joseph make to this?
5. In what kind of situations is it a deep comfort to know that God's purpose stretches far beyond ourselves and our lifetime?

Notes

1. See Melvin Tinker, *Reclaiming Genesis* (Monarch, 2010).
2. D. A. Carson, *For the Love of God,* vol. 1 (Inter-Varsity Press, 1998), entry for 17 February.

3. Cited in Vernon White, *The Fall of a Sparrow – A Concept of Special Divine Action* (Paternoster Press, 1985), p. 111.

4. For the way nomadic peoples passed on stories and traditions, ensuring reliability and continuity, see K. E. Bailey, 'Informal Controlled Oral Tradition and the Synoptic Gospels', *Themelios* 20.2 (1995), < http:// s3.amazonaws.com/tgc-documents/journal-issues/20.2_Bailey.pdf>.

5. Basil Mitchell, 'Theology and Falsification', in A. Flew and A. MacIntyre (eds.), *New Essays in Philosophical Theology* (SCM, 1958).

5. PROVIDENCE AND THE INDIVIDUAL
(Psalm 139)

George Mueller was one of the most outstanding Christians of the nineteenth century. He was a man who passionately believed that God was in control over every detail of our lives for our ultimate good and his supreme glory. Together with his wife he set up orphanages to care for hundreds of children. They lived 'by faith' such that they never made a public appeal for money but prayed to the Lord to provide, which he invariably did. In other words, Mueller really did believe in what Christians call 'providence'. However, in July 1850 his only daughter, Lydia, was struck down with typhoid fever and found herself on the brink of death. How does a Christian father deal with something like that?

This is how Mueller records his experience:

> While I was in this affliction, this great affliction, besides being at peace, so far as the Lord's dispensation was concerned, I also felt perfectly at peace with regard to the *cause* of the affliction. Once on a former occasion, the

hand of the Lord was heavily laid on me and my family. I had not the least
hesitation in knowing, that it was the Father's rod, applied in infinite
wisdom and love, for the restoration of my soul from a state of
lukewarmness. At this time however, I had no such feeling. Conscious as
I was of manifold weaknesses, failings, and shortcomings . . . yet I was
assured that this affliction was not upon me in the way of the fatherly rod,
but for the trial of my faith . . . parents know what an only child, a beloved
child is, and what to believing parents as an only child, a believing child
must be. Well, the Father in heaven said, as it were, by this dispensation,
'Art thou willing to give up this child to me?' My heart responded, 'As it
seems good to Thee, my heavenly Father. Thy will be done.' But as our
hearts were made willing to give back our beloved child to him who had
given her to us, so he was ready to leave her to us and she lived . . . Of all
the trials of faith that as yet I have had to pass through, this was the
greatest, and by God's abundant mercy, I own it to his praise, I was
enabled to delight myself in the will of God; for I felt perfectly sure, that,
if the Lord took this beloved daughter, it would be best for her parents,
best for herself, and more for the glory of God than if she lived . . . [1]

It would be all too easy to think that Mueller could say such a thing
after his daughter had recovered but may well have been singing quite
a different tune had she died. Possibly, but I doubt it given his
response to the death of his wife. Mary Mueller died of rheumatic
fever after they had been married for thirty-four years. Mueller
preached at her funeral laying out three points, his third being, 'The
Lord was good and did good in taking her from me'. Under this point
he related how he had prayed for her during her illness:

Yes, my Father, the times of my darling wife are in Thy hands. Thou wilt
do the very best thing for her and for me, whether life or death. If it may
be, raise up yet again my precious wife, Thou art able to do it, though she
is so ill; but whatsoever Thou dealest with me, only help me to continue
to be perfectly satisfied with thy Holy will.

Then looking back on the way God responded to this prayer he said,

Everyday I see more and more how great is her loss to the orphans.
Yet, without an effort, my inmost soul habitually joys in the joy of
that loved departed one. Her happiness gives joy to me. My dear
daughter and I would not have her back, were it possible to produce
it by the turn of a hand. God himself has done it; we are satisfied
with Him.[2]

It is quite clear from these reflections that Mueller was acting
upon the belief that God is good, wise and all powerful and as such
answers prayer. *After* the event, Mueller looks back with gratitude
and can see God's hand at work, but *during* the event he still believes
God's hand is at work and trusts him for the outcome. It is obvious
that during the dreadfully taxing time of their daughter's illness,
George and Mary Mueller were also remembering other times when
God was providentially at work, weaving a pattern in their lives
which was often mysterious but never senseless, which in turn gave
them strength to cope with their present crisis. This is especially
when belief in providence comes into its own.

The seventeenth century Puritan minister, John Flavel wrote: 'It
is the duty of the saints, especially in times of straights, to reflect
upon the performances of Providence for them in all the states and
through all the stages of their lives.'[3] This extends not only to the
time we were born but even before that, while we were in our
mother's womb. Everything we are, everything we have, is connected
to everything else: the parents we had, the friends we made, the
country in which we were born; all of these fall within the personal
care of God in order for him to bring about his good and perfect
will in our lives. One passage in the Bible which perhaps more than
any other focuses this truth for us is Psalm 139.

The God who perplexes

Psalms can broadly be divided into two types, praise and lament.
The question arises: into which category does this psalm fall? Is this

a 'hallelujah' psalm or a 'Lord-why-is this-happening-to-me?' psalm?
The indications are that it is the latter.[4] It is evident looking at verses
19–22 that David's enemies are giving him a hard time and he
wants God to act swiftly to sort them out but can't quite understand
why God seems to be so slow in responding,

> If only you would slay the wicked, O God!
>   Away from me, you bloodthirsty men!
> They speak of you with evil intent;
>   your adversaries misuse your name.
> Do I not hate those who hate you, O LORD,
>   and abhor those who rise up against you?
> I have nothing but hatred for them;
>   I count them my enemies.

Remember how George Mueller said that there were times in his
Christian life when he could see God using hardship as a way of
discipling him because he had drifted? So it is here that David is in
effect saying to God that while he is far from perfect, there is nothing
in his life *at the moment* as far as he can see which merits this kind of
corrective treatment. He doesn't believe that it is because he needs
to be disciplined that such things are happening for he almost challenges God to get out the magnifying glass in order to examine him:
'Search me, O God, and know my heart; test me and know my
anxious thoughts. See if there is any offensive way in me, and lead
me in the way everlasting' (vv. 23–24). The verb 'to search' (*ḥāqar*)
is used of miners digging into the earth in search for ore (Job 28:3)
and of explorers spying out the land (Judg. 18:2).[5] It's as if David is
throwing down the gauntlet, 'Probe as deeply as you want Lord, but
you will not find offences in me which justify what is occurring at
the moment. Help me quickly!'
    Similarly with the start of the psalm:

> O LORD, you have searched me
>   and you know me.

You know when I sit and when I rise;
   you perceive my thoughts from afar.
You discern my going out and my lying down;
   you are familiar with all my ways.
Before a word is on my tongue
   you know it completely, O LORD.
You hem me in – behind and before;
   you have laid your hand upon me.
Such knowledge is too wonderful for me,
   too lofty for me to attain (vv. 1–6).

The verb translated, 'hem me in' or 'hedge me in' is used in other passages in an oppressive rather than protective sense (it is used, for example, to describe the laying of a siege). Job uses slightly different terminology but likewise speaks of 'hemming' in negative terms (Job 3:23; 7:12). David is fully aware that God knows all things, including the psalmist's thoughts and words, even before they are verbalized.

Therefore, since God is omniscient, he knows that David hasn't done anything wrong to warrant the vicious attacks of these men. Yet it is because he believes that God not only knows all things but is in control of all things he believes that in some way God is behind this trial, hence his saying he feels hemmed in *by God* and experiences the weight of *God's* hand upon him through these tough circumstances. Indeed, so crushing is David's experience that he even considers it an attractive possibility to run away from it all, including escaping from God:

Where can I go from your Spirit?
   Where can I flee from your presence?
If I go up to the heavens, you are there;
   if I make my bed in the depths, you are there.
If I rise on the wings of the dawn,
   if I settle on the far side of the sea,
even there your hand will guide me,
   your right hand will hold me fast.

If I say, 'Surely the darkness will hide me
    and the light become night around me,'
even the darkness will not be dark to you;
    the night will shine like the day,
      for darkness is as light to you (Ps. 139:7–12).

The God who is present

Here David engages in what today would be called a 'thought experiment'. What would be the outcome of *not* being in God's presence? Maybe it would be possible to blast off into the highest point of the stratosphere and outdistance God? Or dive into the deepest parts of the ocean and find God absent? Perhaps it is possible to outrun God by going so far east as to fly off with the morning light as it wings its way over the continents and continues west beyond the bounds of the sea? But the very thought reveals the absurdity of it all, for the God who knows everything is the God who is *everywhere;* he is omniscient and omnipresent.

Have you ever felt like that? It has to be admitted that things must be pretty dire for David to want this. However, he submits to what he knows to be true, namely, that it is not possible to escape from God (and why would we ultimately want to?). If you find yourself in the darkness, who better to have by your side than the one who can see into that darkness? There is still hope that God's hand will guard and guide you, even if though at the moment it feels that hand is against you.

It is important to note that David doesn't take the apparently easy way out that many today are doing by saying, 'God is limited you know. In order to respect human freedom even *he* doesn't know what is going to happen in the future. He might try and turn things around after the fact, but God is as frustrated by events as the next man. God can't be blamed for what is happening to me, he is just doing his best. The trouble is, his best isn't good enough.'[6] Not at all! It is *because* David believes in the absolute sovereignty of God and overruling providence that he prays in the way he does. He knows that God in some way is behind all the difficult things that are going on in his life at the moment, which is why he is trying to wrestle with God's purposes in them and pleads with God to do something about them. It is because he is aware that God is the perfect judge and knows all and sees all, that he finds himself in a bit of a quandary: David is innocent and the other men guilty so why does God delay in bringing about justice? David does not abandon his belief in God's sovereignty; he wrestles with it and works it through, allowing great thoughts of God to provide the firm anchor for his soul when the going gets rough. And we are to do the same.

The God who is powerful

It is the thoughts which appear at the centre of the psalm which provide such tender strength when we begin to think that life is simply too much to cope with and that God has somehow lost control:

> For you created my inmost being;
>> you knit me together in my mother's womb.
> I praise you because I am fearfully and wonderfully made;
>> your works are wonderful,
>> I know that full well.
> My frame was not hidden from you
>> when I was made in the secret place.
> When I was woven together in the depths of the earth,
>> your eyes saw my unformed body.
> All the days ordained for me
>> were written in your book
>> before one of them came to be.
> How precious to me are your thoughts, O God!
>> How vast is the sum of them!

Were I to count them,
  they would outnumber the grains of sand.
When I awake,
  I am still with you (vv.13–18).

We may think: 'Surely, if ever there was a time I was not known to God, when I *was* hidden from him, it was while I was in the womb. How can a microscopic ball of cells travelling on its mysterious journey down the fallopian tube be of any interest to God? Why, even my mother was not aware of my existence then, so how could God be?' That is the sort of question David is pondering. Never having seen an ultrascan does not prevent him from using the most sublime figurative language to describe God's providential care in piecing us together to become the people he designed us to be. 'You created me,' intones David, 'like a potter shaping a vessel. You knit me like a weaver blending together threads in a complex tapestry.' When David exclaims, 'I am wonderfully made', the word he uses *(ruqamtî)* is a very interesting one. One translation renders it, 'You painted me with a needle.' Like some rich embroidery made of nerves and blood vessels, that is how skilfully God personally superintended our coming into being inside our mother's womb.

'How precious to me are your thoughts, O God! How vast is the sum of them! Were I to count them, they would outnumber the grains of sand' (v. 17). It would appear that David is referring to God's pre-natal thoughts about him, all the details that have gone into making him the man he is: eye colour, hair texture, height, weight, IQ, his fear of spiders; millions, if not trillions, of thoughts have come together in perfect harmony to produce this glorious creature called a human being, more specifically, me.

Of course, we are in a better position than David to know how wonderfully made we are and such knowledge is meant to move us to worship and awe. Take our brain for example. We are talking about two handfuls of tissue, weighing a little more than three pounds (about 1.5 kg), with the colour and something of the consistency of porridge, which is our equipment for feeling, speaking, seeing, smelling, appreciating art, remembering, enjoying sex, doing crosswords and a hundred and one other activities that make up our daily lives. Isn't it extraordinary that through this bundle of 'stuff' we are able 'in here' to get an accurate picture of what is 'out there'? The human brain contains ten thousand million nerve cells, each cell connected to ten thousand others. This means that if you could make a model of the brain using cells the size of a volume of the *Encyclopaedia Britannica* you would need nearly the whole of the earth's surface in which to lay it out! Awesome is a word which hardly does justice to this reality.

The point is, we are not to take these truths for granted. By that I don't simply mean that we are to be thankful that we can see, touch, speak and think, though we should, but rather to appreciate that all of this comes from God's personal and specific say-so. Personally God gave me the right kinds of biological material to be the person he wanted me to be in order to know him and serve him in the world the way he intended. This should help us in moving towards Christian contentment. You may like to be taller but you are the height you are. You might like to have blue eyes but you have the eyes you have. Why do you want to be what you are not? We might further ask: why do you think it will make the slightest difference if some of your physical details could be changed? A forty-five-year-old American cosmetic surgery advisor gushed to the *Sunday Times* a while ago about her ten-year 'marathon surgery' in pursuit of new beauty. She had the works: eyes, nose, chin, tummy and knees, that was just for starters, she had more plastic than a Tupperware party! At the end of it all she said, 'This is the real me. I felt like a misfit in my old face and body; it never felt right. This is the way I want to live, and I couldn't do it with my old face and body, I don't even want to associate myself with that person. She is dead. I cut her up.' Do we honestly think that she became a less vain and selfish person because she had a new nose and chin?

From the vantage point of eternity my whole life was mapped out by you, says David; all the decisions I would ever freely make, from which shoes I would wear to which wife I would choose were foreordained by you, 'All the days ordained for me were written in your book before one of them came to be' (v. 16). God knew exactly when I was to enter this world; what is more, he knows exactly when I am to leave it. This gives life a meaning, as every story has a meaning, a goal towards which it is heading.

Isn't this a truth worth knowing, especially when life hits the hard times? One person who knew this to be so was the Scottish minister George Matheson, who wrote the moving hymn, 'O love that will not let me go', which he composed on the eve of his sister's wedding. His whole family had gone to the wedding and had left him alone. He writes of something which had happened to him that caused immense mental anguish. There is a story of how years before, he had been engaged, until his fiancée learned that he was going blind and there was nothing the doctors could do. As a result of this devastating news, his fiancée told him that she could not go through life with a blind man (he actually went blind while studying for the ministry and his sister had been the one who had taken care of him all these years, but now she was gone). The Lord had richly blessed him in a church where he regularly preached to over 1,500 people each week. But he was only able to do this because of the care of his sister who soon was to be married. The question which began to haunt his mind was: Who will care for him now, a blind man? Not only that, but his sister's marriage brought a fresh reminder of his own heartbreak, jilted by his fiancée because he had gone blind. It was in the midst of this intense sadness that the Lord gave him this hymn – written he says in five minutes! How could he maintain such unwavering hopefulness in the midst of such circumstances and trials? His hymn gives us a clue.

> O Joy, that seekest me through pain,
>   I cannot close my heart to Thee;
> I trace the rainbow through the rain,
> And feel the promise is not vain
>   That morn shall tearless be.

He trusted in God's promises; the God who is all perceiving, all present and all powerful.

From this we are meant to take great strength and move towards praise when we think of God's providence in bringing us to where we are today. Let me share a few personal things which illustrate this.

I am glad that I was brought up as a child in Britain in the 1960s; it really was a great time in which to enjoy childhood. I have appreciated the fact that God had me born when I was and, unlike my grandfather, I have not had to live through two World Wars. I am also thankful to God that the comprehensive school system came along just when it did because someone from my solid working-class background would never have gone to grammar school and I would never have proceeded to university at a time when only 2% of the population managed to obtain a place. It was great to be a student in the 70s and 80s too. Every time I go to the dentist I am so grateful that I wasn't born 300 years ago, for not only would I probably not have any teeth at all by now but they would have been extracted in a very painful way. I am appreciative of the medical care we have in Britain in contrast to the lack of free care which my Granddad was subject to, such that when as a boy he ate some laburnum seeds he was seriously ill to the point of death and all he had to depend upon was my Great-Grandmother tending him with herbs. What is more, although I wasn't brought up in a Christian home I was raised in a stable home which had standards which kept me on the straight and narrow. Therefore, I thank God for the parents he gave me and if you have Christian parents how much more should you thank him?

Have you thought about how privileged those of us are who have been born and raised in Britain? I know grumbling is a British pastime but we should be more cautious and restrained in doing that given God's providential ruling of our country over the years. As a nation we have been singularly blessed by God in the past. For a thousand years Christianity has been the official faith of this land. We have been protected from paganism in the distant past, from Islam in the Middle Ages, from a corrupt Roman Catholicism in the sixteenth century and from fascist and Marxist dictatorships in the twentieth century. Christianity gave us our schools, hospitals, prison reforms and factory acts. Blessing upon blessing has come our way.

It is theoretically possible that we could have been born in Pakistan or North Korea. From a merely human point of view, what would have been the chances of becoming a Christian in such places? The answer is, very slim indeed. What is more, if we had become a Christian in such countries we would be persecuted. Is it not a cause for wonderment and gratitude to the providence of God that he placed us in a country which is politically stable and where there are still many freedoms we enjoy, including the freedom to believe?

But even after all of this you might say, 'It is all right for God up in the heavens to rule over all things where it is safe and secure, but it is pretty rough for us down here', hence David's complaint. However, when we bear in mind that God subjected himself to his own providence in this world such a complaint collapses like a flimsy stack of cards. For the Christian turning to this psalm can say God knows how all of this feels too, from the inside. As a descendent of David, Jesus the Son of God went through all of this. In the womb of Mary, *God* was a ball of cells rapidly multiplying. *God* saw through the newly formed eyes of a developing embryo. *God* felt what it was like to touch with a baby's hand.

Pondering this, Augustine of Hippo expressed his sense of wonder in this way:

> He [God the Son], through whom time was made, was made in time; and He, older by eternity than the world itself, was younger in age than many of His servants in the world; He, who made man, was made man; He was given existence by a mother whom He brought into existence; He was carried in hands which He formed; He nursed at breasts which He filled; He cried like a babe in the manger in speechless infancy – this Word without which human eloquence is speechless![7]

This also meant that *God* knew what it was like to be born under a tyrannical political regime and a corrupt religion. As he walked this earth, God the Son rejoiced in the thought of his heavenly Father knowing when he sat and when he stood, when he slept and when he ate. Even in the dark night of Gethsemane he knew that his Father was still watching him and his way was not hidden from him. Jesus Christ was born at just the right time in the right place; his days were all written in his Father's book, nothing was ever outside his eternal will and good purpose. As the rejected King hung on a cross, he was surrounded by bloodthirsty men. It was his Father's will that he be raised from the dead and set to rule over the lives of his children moment by moment.

Isn't it a wonderfully comforting thought that this is the God we worship and have come to know in the Lord Jesus? Isn't it a liberating contrast to the pagan way of thinking that our lives are tossed about by impersonal chance and fate? Here we are to draw strength from the belief that there is Someone not only watching over us, but lovingly at work in us, through us and all around us, writing a story with our lives which will count in eternity.

Questions for reflection and discussion

1. 'It is the duty of the saints, especially in times of straights, to reflect upon the performances of Providence for them in all the states and through all the stages of their lives' (John Flavel). Take some time to reflect on God's providence in the different stages of your life.

2. Reflect on Psalm 139:13–18. Whether you view yourself with high esteem or low esteem, how should God's creating providence shape how you view yourself? How will it impact how we value other people?

3. What are some of the blessings of God's providence that you and your church family may take for granted?

4. How is God's providence a part of the good news we have to share with unbelievers?

Notes

1. Cited by John Piper in *The Pleasures of God* (Mentor-Christian Focus, 2009), p. 182.

2. Piper, *Pleasures of God*, p. 184.

3. John Flavel, *The Mystery of Providence* (Banner of Truth Trust, 1991), p. 60.

4. See John H. Walton, 'Hebrew Corner 5: "hedge" (Psalm 139)', <http:// www.koinoniablog.net/2008/09/ hebrew-corner-5.html>.

5. See Steven C. Roy, *How Much Does God Foreknow? A Comprehensive Biblical Study* (Apollos, 2006), p. 28.

6. Notwithstanding objections to the contrary, this is arguably the end position of those who advocate the 'openness of God' viewpoint, see Clark Pinnock *et al.*, *The Openness of God: A Biblical Challenge to the Traditional Understanding of God* (InterVarsity Press, 1994).

7. Augustine, sermon 187.

6. PROVIDENCE AND PRAYER

One of the most wonderful mysteries in the universe is that prayer changes things, that is, we can ask God to do things and things get done as a result of prayer which otherwise wouldn't happen.[1] In his wisdom God has so arranged his world that we have the ability to make significant choices, some good and some bad, which affect the course of history. One of the means God has given us to make our choices really count is through prayer, asking God to act. Because God is all wise and all powerful, the one who is able to know 'the end from the beginning' (Isa. 46:10), he is able to weave those requests into his eternal good purposes. Our prayers are superintended by him together with everything else in creation.

It is at this point that our thinking can seriously go astray in one of two directions.

The first is to say, 'If God is all powerful, all knowing and all good, and if everything is preordained, then he is going to do whatever he wills anyway and so our prayers can't have any significant effect. They may help us psychologically, such that by talking to God we get things off our chest which might make us feel better, but they don't count for much in the big scheme of things. Prayer, then, at rock bottom, is fake – so why bother?' Here the emphasis is on God being absolutely sovereign.

The second route, although different to the first, ends up in the same place, namely, denying the usefulness of prayer, but for a different reason. Here the objection is: 'If human beings are free to make up their own minds then God can't be absolutely sovereign; he must take risks such that human decisions can thwart his purposes, and so there are severe limits to what we can ask for without undermining human freedom. If, for example, you have been praying for your sister to become a Christian and God has done everything he can to bring her to himself, but somehow she won't surrender to him, why bother asking God to save her? Isn't it out of order to pressure God to do more when there is no more he can do? So just give up on prayer.'[2] Here the emphasis is upon a certain understanding of human freedom (libertarian).

Taken at face value, both objections appear to have some force, but only because they employ a strange 'logic' which goes beyond the Bible. It is always foolish (and dangerous) to play up one aspect of what the Bible teaches at the expense of something else it equally affirms. As we have been seeing, the God of the Bible is presented as the one who does rule over all; he is all knowing, all wise and all powerful and is not caught out by anything we may think or do. On the other hand, human beings are presented as responsible, conscious moral agents who make significant choices, doing what we desire to do (freedom of inclination). God has chosen to relate to us personally without compromising the fact that he is God (working all things according to the counsel of his will), but he does respond to us as a result of the agency of prayer, for he is 'God-in-relationship'. And so, although as within any language applied to God it needs to be qualified,[3] we do find Scripture describing the Sovereign God as 'repenting' or 'relenting' as a result of people praying.[4] There are plenty of examples of this, but let us look at one which is very striking. We find it in Exodus 32 where Moses prays to God. At this point in salvation-history, the people of Israel have already broken the Ten Commandments, which had just been given to them, by building and worshipping a golden calf and engaging in an orgy. God is so incensed that he says he will wipe them out, '"I have seen these people," the LORD said to Moses, "and they are a stiff-necked people. Now leave me alone so that my anger may burn against them and that I may destroy them. Then I will make you into a great nation"' (vv. 9–10). But Moses steps into the breach and reminds God of his promises, arguing that his reputation will be brought into disrepute for saying one thing, 'I will save the people', and doing another, destroying them, let alone appearing to renege on his promises to Abraham. Moses appeals to God as the sovereign king to show mercy (vv. 11–13). And that is exactly what happened: 'Then the LORD relented and did not bring on his people the disaster he had threatened' (Exod. 32:14).[5]

The theoretical problem raised by the belief in the efficacy of prayer to a sovereign God is acknowledged by C. S. Lewis, who helpfully places it within the wider context of God using certain means to achieve desired ends:

Can we believe that God really modifies his action in response to the suggestions of men? For infinite wisdom does not need telling what is best, and infinite goodness needs no urging to do it. But neither does God need any of those things that are done by finite agents, whether living or inanimate. He could, if he chose, repair our bodies miraculously without food; or give us food without the aid of farmers, bakers, and butchers; or knowledge without the aid of learned men; or convert the heathen without missionaries. Instead he allows soils and weather and animals and the muscles, minds and wills of men to co-operate in the execution of his will. 'God,' said Pascal, 'instituted prayer in order to lend to his creatures the dignity of causality.' But not only prayer; whenever we act at all he lends us that dignity. It is not really stranger, nor less strange, that my prayers should affect the course of events than that my other actions should do so. They have not advised or changed God's mind – that is, his over-all purpose. But that purpose will be realised in different ways according to the actions, including prayers, of his creatures.[6]

Our problem in trying to see how prayer can 'work' is because we often have the wrong view of God in relation to his world. More often than not we slip into a view of God as portrayed in the film *Bruce Almighty*, with God sitting in a celestial office feverishly dealing one at a time with all the prayer requests which come in: Mrs Green prays that her husband's cancer be cured, Mr Young prays his wife might conquer alcoholism, and so on, with millions more worthy requests. In principle it is in line with what God wills for his creation that Mr Green be healthy and Mrs Young be sober. But what if both get worse? Does this mean that God doesn't answer prayer?

The tangled web of human affairs living in a fallen and broken world like ours makes things rather more complex. Sometimes the good ends God desires come out of certain evils. So at one level, cancer is an evil, as is all sickness, which is part of the curse upon the rebellious world in which we all live. God does sometimes answer prayers for healing (and in one sense all healing is divine in that God is working providentially). But we also have to recognize that since we are mortal, all people die sometime. What is more, other prayers may be offered and answered which can *only* be answered if there is *not* healing, like gaining patience through suffering and an increased focus on the world to come. Maybe Mr Green's son has turned his back on God, and that it will be through his father's illness that he will come to his senses and return. God knows this and so in order to 'answer' one prayer, the return of the son, he doesn't 'answer' the other prayer, complete healing. God alone knows what is best.[7]

Because God stands outside time, he, as it were, can hear all the prayers ever made, and ever will be made, in an eternal moment and use each one of them outside time to bring about his good purposes within time. He is able to view the whole course of human history – past, present and future – together in the eternal present and weave all our decisions freely made into a pattern which is his.[8]

Therefore we are called to pray as Jesus prayed. As a result of our prayers some things will happen which, if we had not prayed, would not have happened and we are responsible for whether we pray or don't pray. Because God is a personal God he invites us to share in his work by praying. As Bruce Ware puts it, 'God has devised prayer as a means of enlisting us as participants in the work he has ordained, as part of the outworking of his sovereign rulership over all . . . the relationship between divine sovereignty and petitionary prayer can be stated by this word: *participation*.'[9]

Because God is transcendent and infinite he has the power and the wisdom to use our prayers as he sees fit to do things which we could never imagine. If he were not all powerful, then there would be little point in praying. If he were not all wise it would be dangerous to pray; after all, who wants to ask of an all-powerful but foolish, myopic Being to do things? But God is *both* perfectly wise and infinitely powerful which is why we can pray with confidence.

A proper recognition

The relation between providence and prayer is brought together in the opening words of what we call the Lord's Prayer: 'Our Father in heaven' (Matt. 6:9).

The one true God is the God 'in heaven'. This emphasizes his transcendence, his 'otherness', a God who is vastly superior and different to all that he has made, one who is infinite, without beginning and without end, glorious in his majestic beauty, and Lord of the universe. The world and its creatures are contingent upon God, not the other way around. He is the source of all goodness and kindness, whose creative genius conceived and fashioned this vast and complex universe which we are discovering more and more about each day. He is the one who knows all things, knowing everything that has happened at every point in the cosmos and what will happen at every point in creation right into the future (that is, the future from our standpoint). It is this vision of God, such that the furthest stretches of outer space are within his reach, which forms the springboard for praise in Psalm 104:

O Lord my God, you are very great;
    you are clothed with splendour and majesty.
He wraps himself in light as with a garment;
    he stretches out the heavens like a tent (vv. 1–2).

Yet at the same time he is personally involved in the caring supervision of all life on earth:

He makes springs pour water into the ravines;
    it flows between the mountains.
They give water to all the beasts of the field;
    the wild donkeys quench their thirst.
The birds of the air nest by the waters (vv. 10–12).

Recent findings make our belief in the God who is in heaven and who fills the heavens even more breathtaking. For example, the Ant nebula in our galaxy is a cloud of gas which is three to six thousand light years from Earth. The Cone nebula is 2600 light years from Earth – that is 35 thousand million return trips to the moon. Someone has described the heavens as 'God's workshop'. And so it is here that we see something of the divine artistry, the super-craftsman, at work, who, according to our psalmist, unfolds all of this as easily as a man opening up a small tent to sleep in. It is that simple for God. This is the One Jesus tells us is 'Our Father in heaven'. Does this not cause us to pause and ask a few questions? If God is able to place the stars in their sockets and suspend the heavens like a curtain, do we think it is remotely possible that God is able to guide our life? If God is so almighty that he is able to ignite the sun as easily as we might strike a match, could it be that he has enough light to lighten our path when things seem dark? In each case the answer is going to be 'yes'. Jesus certainly thought so, for he goes on after teaching about prayer to teach about provision:

Therefore I tell you, do not worry about your life, what you will eat or drink; or about your body, what you will wear. Is not life more important than food, and the body more important than clothes? Look at the birds of the air; they do not sow or reap or store away in barns, and yet your *heavenly Father* feeds them. Are you not much more valuable than they? Who of you by worrying can add a single hour to his life? (Matt. 6:25–27)

This much would have been affirmed by any first-century Jew, maybe even more so. They often thought of God as being so exalted that he seemed rather remote. It was his distance rather than his nearness which was emphasized. Not surprisingly some people today wonder if a God who is so busy with such major projects as bringing nebulas into being in the outer reaches of the galaxy could possibly be concerned with their humdrum affairs in the inner sanctum of their home: 'Why should God who is so great be bothered with someone like me who is so small?' Although we may be so familiar with the term that we take it for granted, Jesus' first hearers would have been stunned by the answer he gave as to 'why?' when he said that his followers were now in a position to call this God, 'Father'. Jesus tells them to pray to the One who is '*Our* Father in heaven'.

A personal relationship

Sadly, not everyone has a positive experience of their fathers. Some have suffered abuse of one kind or another and still bear the scars, emotional or physical. As a result, some find it very difficult to think of God as 'father' in any positive, affectionate sense. But even here, those who have tragically suffered know deep down that there *is* a model of fatherhood, a standard, which their own fathers have failed to reach. That standard is God himself. He is the perfect Father who will not abuse, manipulate or cajole for his own selfish ends, for he is always other-person centred, never self-centred. All that the best of our fathers could ever be, God is and infinitely more. Does a father care? So does God (Luke 12: 6–7). Does a father order things for the good of his family? So does God (Rom. 8:28). Does a father exercise loving discipline, withholding what is good from us in order to give us what is best? So does God (Heb. 12:7–13). Does a father listen to his children at whatever age they are: the gurgling of a baby, the stammering of a toddler, the pleadings of a teenager, the respect-ful musings of an adult? So does God as we make our way through the spiritual equivalent of the seven ages of man (Luke 11:1–13). But there is one vital difference; this is *God* our Father, the one who is in heaven. It is the coming together of 'Father' and 'in heaven' which makes all the difference in the world to God hearing and answering our prayers as he providentially works out his purposes in our lives.

God is untainted by the atmosphere of sin, for he is holy. He is unbridled by the timeline of history, for he is infinite. He is un-hindered by the weariness of the body, for he is spirit. What controls our earthly fathers does not control him. What troubles us doesn't trouble him. This is how the writer Max Lucado captures these thoughts:

> Is an eagle troubled by a traffic jam? Hardly, he soars above it. Is a whale panicked by a hurricane? No, he plunges beneath it. How much more is God our Father able to soar above or plunge beneath the troubles of earth? Our questions betray our lack of understanding. How is God able to sort between the different and often competing claims upon him – the farmer wants rain for the crops, the family wants sun for the picnic? Who says that God hasn't the wisdom to decide which needs are greater and which actions will best serve his loving purposes for his people?[10]

But we may yet say, 'Yes, but I still find it difficult to see how God can be sovereign and yet personally respond to my prayers in his providential workings.' Interestingly enough all the evidence is that Jesus himself had no such difficulty. A few chapters later in Matthew's Gospel we hear Jesus praying these words, 'I praise you, *Father, Lord of heaven and earth*.' (Here Jesus affirms God's personal nearness, he is 'Father', and also his greatness, he is 'Lord of heaven and earth'.) Why such praise?

Because you have hidden these things from the wise and learned, and revealed them to little children. Yes, Father, for this was your good pleasure. All things have been committed to me by my Father. No one knows the Son except the Father, and no one knows the Father except the Son and those to whom the Son chooses to reveal him (Matt. 11:25–27).

Here God's sovereignty is underscored. He has hidden some things from those who in their pride think they know it all, but has revealed things to the open and responsive, those who act like little children; in this way he is like a Father. Then comes the invitation which emphasizes our choice and personal responsibility:

Come to me, all you who are weary and burdened, and I will give you rest. Take my yoke upon you and learn from me, for I am gentle and humble in heart, and you will find rest for your souls. For my yoke is easy and my burden is light (Matt 11:28–30).

In other words, Jesus held these twin truths together and refused to fall prey to the temptation of playing one off against the other, and surely that should be our approach too.

Powerful prayer

For us to know that God is our Father and at the same time the great God of the universe should result in powerful prayer. Let us go to one of the very first prayer meetings in the early church to see how this might be so.

It has been a tough time; two of the leading apostles, Peter and John, have been beaten up and threatened with more of the same if they keep on telling people about God's saving love in Jesus Christ. How do they respond? Well, they don't throw up their hands in despair saying, 'This is obviously God's will' and fatefully resign themselves to going into hiding. Nor do they say, 'God can't contradict the freedom of the rulers so what is the point of praying?'

Instead they pray to the God who rules over all, asking him to give them the strength to be obedient to him:

> They raised their voices together in prayer to God. 'Sovereign Lord,' they said, 'you made the heaven and the earth and the sea, and everything in them. You spoke by the Holy Spirit through the mouth of your servant, our father David:
>
> > '"Why do the nations rage
> >   and the peoples plot in vain?
> > The kings of the earth take their stand
> >   and the rulers gather together
> > against the Lord
> >   and against his anointed one."
>
> 'Indeed Herod and Pontius Pilate met together with the Gentiles and the people of Israel in this city to conspire against your holy servant Jesus, whom you anointed. They did what your power and will had decided beforehand should happen. Now, Lord, consider their threats and enable your servants to speak your word with great boldness. Stretch out your hand to heal and perform miraculous signs and wonders through the name of your holy servant Jesus.' (Acts 4:24–30)

There we have it, divine sovereignty and human responsibility lying side by side without any hint of embarrassment or apology. On the basis that God *is* in control and is passionately involved in his world, caring for his people, they take their responsibilities seriously and ask God to act, more specifically to give them courage to keep on sharing the Christian message. We see the result of this kind of prayer in what happened next: 'After they prayed, the place where they were meeting was shaken. And they were all filled with the Holy Spirit and spoke the word of God boldly' (Acts 4:30). Their heavenly Father answered their prayers. Working *with* God, prayer and proclamation are the means he uses by his Holy Spirit to bring about his will in people being brought into a saving relationship with himself.

It is because God is Almighty, the God in heaven and of the heavens, that he *can* answer us when we pray. It is because he is our Father that he *wants* to hear us when we pray, out of concern for our needs and in an intimate relationship with us. Our responsibility is not to try and work out *how* this can be so, but believe *that* it is so and pray.

Questions for reflection and discussion

1. If somebody asked you why you pray, how would you answer?
2. Are there things that you are tempted not to pray about because you feel God can't affect them?
3. How does describing prayer as 'participation' impact how you view prayer?
4. Do you see God as far off, or near? What difference does the relationship between providence and prayer have on this? What advice might you give to someone who feels God is far off?
5. Think about how the providence of God might shape your priorities in terms of what you pray, how you pray and when you pray.

Notes

1. 'You do not have because you do not ask God' (Jas 4:2); 'The prayer of a righteous man is powerful and effective' (Jas 5:16). Such verses are to be seen alongside other verses which are equally emphatic in Scripture concerning 'prevenient grace', e.g. 'Before they call I will answer, while they are still speaking I will hear' (Isa. 65:24).
2. This is the objection Roger Nicole raises against Gregory Boyd's theological position called 'open theism': 'In terms of Boyd's view of human free will, it would be wholly nugatory to pray for the conversion of anybody. This would be an area where God is already doing the best

he can do, in view of his alleged universal saving will. To bring a person to conversion, what would be needed is to address this individual's free will in order to induce repentance and faith, and this is the area into which God allegedly refuses to intervene lest he violate the will of the creature. One could not refrain from noting that it was fortunate that Monica was not carried away by this logic and that she kept praying for her son Augustine's conversion until it occurred. Surely it is important to challenge people directly to repentance and faith, but in view of human depravity this challenge would remain ineffective unless God himself should work in the depths of personality to bring about the new birth' (Roger Nicole, in *Reformation & Revival* 10/1, Winter 2001, review of Gregory A. Boyd, *God of the Possible: A Biblical Introduction to the Open View of God* [Baker Publishing Co, 2001]).

3. There are passages which state categorically that God does *not* repent or change his mind (1 Sam. 15:29 and Num. 23:19) and so one needs to coordinate these passages with others which do suggest a change of heart on God's part in such a way that Scripture is not presented as contradicting itself or misrepresenting God's nature and his relation to the world. For one such helpful presentation see, Steven C. Roy, *How Much does God Know? A Comprehensive Study* (Apollos, 2006), ch. 4, 'A Different View of Divine Foreknowledge', pp. 125–194.

4. The Hebrew word translated 'repent', *nāḥam*, could be rendered 'relent', as is often the case in the NIV. This casts a different shade of meaning on what is happening in such cases. Rather than God changing his purpose it can be viewed as God changing his *attitude* towards those he has warned and prayer is instrumental in this.

5. For a very helpful discussion on the sovereignty of God and prayer see D. A. Carson, *A Call to Spiritual Reformation* (Inter-Varsity Press, 1992), ch. 9, 'A Sovereign and Personal God'. Carson rightly notes: 'The perverse and the unbeliever will appeal to God's sovereignty to urge the futility of prayer in a determined universe; they will appeal to passages depicting God as a person (including those that speak of him relenting) to infer that he is weak, fickle and impotent, once again concluding that it is useless to pray. But the faithful will insist that, properly handled, both God's sovereignty and his personhood become reasons for more

prayer, not reasons for abandoning prayer. It is worth praying to a sovereign God because he is free and can take action as he wills; it is worth praying to a personal God because he hears, responds, and acts on behalf of his people, not according to blind rigidities of inexorable fate', p. 165.

6. C. S. Lewis, 'The Efficacy of Prayer', in *Fern Seeds and Elephants* (Fount, 1975), pp. 101–102. The understanding of the role of prayer in relation to God's sovereign plan which is being adopted in this chapter is to see prayers as valid secondary causes which God has instituted and deemed necessary to achieve his purposes.

7. See Harry Blamires, *On Christian Truth* (Servant Books, 1983), ch. 8, p. 39.

8. Here we have to take into account the different logical standpoints involved, those of the Creator-in-eternity and the creature-in-time: 'Once we are in a position from which (retrospectively) the Creator's eye-view is meaningful to us, then it is not only the answer to prayer, but *also our asking,* which are seen to be "according to the determinate counsel" (Acts 2:23 AV). It becomes luminously evident that in general "had we not prayed", things *could* have turned out otherwise; for from this standpoint "had we not. . . " means "had the Creator conceived the drama differently" and once we say this, we can use no firm inferences to prescribe or proscribe the outcome, for our only firm ground of inference is the drama as the Creator *has* conceived it, together with his promise to be faithful to that conception (e.g. to Noah in Genesis 8:22).' (Donald M. MacKay, 'The Sovereignty of God in the Natural World', in *The Open Mind and Other Essays*, ed. Melvin Tinker [Inter-Varsity Press, 1988], p. 195).

9. Bruce Ware, 'Prayer and the Sovereignty of God', in Sam Storms and Justin Taylor (eds.), *For the Fame of God's Name – Essays in Honour of John Piper* (Crossway, 2010), p. 138.

10. Max Lucado, *The Great House of God* (W Publishing Group, 1997), p. 41.

7. PROVIDENCE AND GUIDANCE

Do we really believe that God has the best interests of his people at heart and so will guide and direct them? King David certainly did – he writes in Psalm 25:

> Show me your ways, O Lord,
>   teach me your paths;
> guide me in your truth and teach me,
>   for you are my God my Saviour,
>   and my hope is in you all day long . . .
> Good and upright is the Lord;
>   therefore he instructs sinners in his ways.
> He guides the humble in what is right
>   and teaches them his way (vv. 4–5, 8–9).

But this raises a further question: how does God normally guide believers and what part does providence play in that process?

The First Supper

Here is the parable of the 'first supper':[1]

Adam was hungry. He had had a long, challenging day in the Garden of Eden naming animals. His afternoon nap had been refreshing, and his post-siesta introduction to Eve exhilarating, to say the least. But as the sun began to set on the first day, Adam discovered he had worked up an appetite. 'I think we should eat,' he said to Eve. 'Let's call the evening meal "supper".' 'Oh, you're so decisive, Adam,' replied Eve admiringly. 'I like that in a man.' As they discussed how they should proceed, they decided that Adam would gather fruit from the garden, and Eve would prepare the meal. Adam set about his task and soon returned with a basket full of ripe fruit. He gave it to Eve to prepare and went to soak his feet in the soothing current of the Pishon River until supper was ready. He had been reviewing the animals' names for about five minutes when he heard his wife's troubled voice. 'Adam, could you help me for a moment. I'm not sure which of these lovely fruits I should prepare for supper. I've prayed for guidance from the Lord, but I'm not really sure what he wants me to do. I certainly don't want to miss his will on my very first decision. Would you go to the Lord and ask him what I should do about supper?' So Adam left Eve to go to speak with the Lord. Shortly, he returned and appeared perplexed. 'Well?' probed Eve. 'He didn't really answer your question,' replied her husband, 'He just repeated what he said earlier during the garden tour: "From any tree of the garden you may eat freely; but from the tree of the Knowledge of Good and Evil you shall not eat." I assure you Eve, I steered clear of that tree.' 'But that doesn't solve my problem,' said Eve. 'What should I prepare for tonight?' Adam thought for a moment and then said, 'I've never seen such crisp juicy apples. I feel a sense of peace about them. Why don't you prepare them for supper? Maybe while you're getting them ready, you'll experience the same peace I have.' 'All right, Adam,' she agreed. 'I guess you've had more experience in decision making than I have. I appreciate your leadership and will call you when supper's ready.' Adam was only half way back to the river when he heard his wife call a second time, so he jogged back to the clearing where she was working. 'More problems?' he asked. 'Adam, I just can't decide what I should do with these apples. I could dice them, slice them, mash them or bake them in a pie. Or I could just polish them and eat them raw. I really want to be your helper, would you be a dear and go just one more time to the Lord with my problem?' So Adam did as Eve requested. When he returned, he said, 'I got the same answer as before: "From *any* tree of the garden you may eat *freely*; but from the tree of the knowledge of good and evil you shall not eat."' Adam and Eve were both silent for a moment. Then Adam said, 'You know, Eve, the LORD made that statement as though it ought to fully answer my question. I'm sure He could have told me what to eat and how to eat it; but I think He wants *us* to make those decisions. It was the same way with the animals today. He just left their names entirely up to me.' Eve was incredulous. 'Do you mean that it doesn't matter which of these fruits we have for supper? Are you telling me that I *can't* miss God's will in this decision? Adam explained: 'The only way you could do that is to pick some fruit from the forbidden tree. But all of these fruits are all right. Why, I suppose we could eat them all!' Adam snapped his fingers and exclaimed, 'Say, that's a great idea! Let's have fruit salad for supper!' Eve hesitated. 'What's a salad?'

Which 'will' are we talking about?

If you haven't caught on to the significance of that story yet, you soon will. When you think about it, our imaginary Eve in our imaginary scene is very much like many a Christian. She genuinely has a desire to do what is right and, as she puts it, not 'miss out on God's will' for her. But what did she mean exactly? What she was talking about has to be distinguished between the other two senses in which the Bible speaks about the 'will of God'. On the one hand there is God's *sovereign will* in which he is in total control over all things according to his eternal decree and power; this cannot be thwarted. I would suggest that David is resting in *that* sovereign will of God in Psalm 25 which nonetheless did not prevent him from praying to the God who can be entreated simply because he *is* King over all things: 'My eyes are ever on the LORD, for only he will release my feet from the snare. Turn to me and be gracious to me, for I am lonely and afflicted' (vv. 15–16).

On the other hand there is God's 'moral will' which both Adam and Eve knew about in that negative prohibition they were given, stating they should *not* eat from the tree of the knowledge of good and evil. Here the will of God concerns matters of right and wrong which he has revealed to us in the Bible and which we are called to obey. But in addition to these two senses of 'God's will', Eve in our story, and many Christians, speak of God's 'individual will', that is, his personal plan and purpose for their lives. This would cover such matters as: which job to do, who, if anyone, they should marry, which church to attend, which car to buy, or, in Eve's case, which meal to cook! It is this that people are often referring to when they speak of seeking God's guidance for his individual will in their lives. As a consequence they try to look out for certain 'signposts' to indicate in which direction they should be moving, things such as examining personal desires, 'open doors' of opportunity, special guidance with a listening for that 'still small voice' and seeking mature counsel. By lining these up it is hoped to discover God's individual will for them in any a particular matter. We might think of it in terms of the diagram below whereby we try to hit the bull's-eye so we are at the centre of God's will.[2]

The Centre of God's Will

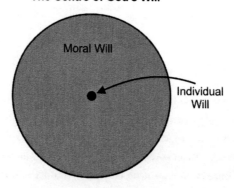

Moral Will

Individual
Will

But there are several problems with this approach, some practical and others theological.

Practically it seems arbitrary, for where do we decide is the cut-off point between 'ordinary decisions' (where I use plain common sense) and really 'important decisions' (where I must know God's will)? Sometimes we find that so-called 'ordinary' decisions and events turn out to be the really important ones, for example missing a train which results in an important meeting, as Bob Bates discovered in our illustration in the first chapter. Also it tends to lead to a lot of unnecessary anxiety, especially amongst those of us who are worriers, leaving us with the nagging question: 'Have I missed God's will for my life and messed things up for ever?' There is also so much uncertainty, how can I *really* know I have got it right and lined up the signposts correctly?

Theologically, it can weaken our hold on the authority of the Bible. God *could* give us extra special revelation if he wanted to, like a dream or a burning bush, but he doesn't *promise* to. However, he *does* promise that the Bible is sufficient for us to live the life he wants us to live: 'All Scripture is God-breathed and is useful for teaching, rebuking, correcting and training in righteousness, so that the man of God may be thoroughly equipped for every good work' (2 Tim. 3:16–17).

There is also the place of wisdom in the Christian life, which the apostle James tells us we are to ask for if we lack it (Jas 1:5). Sometimes the decisions we have to make are not right and wrong decisions, but wise and unwise, the good versus the best. Knowing the difference comes as we develop the skill of applying God's word to the different situations we find ourselves in. Peter Adam describes the role of the Bible in guidance in this way:

> . . . it sets before us the plan of God, God's theological priorities for his people, and the style of obedience which he expects from us. The Bible gives us a framework which sets us free from being the victim of circumstances . . . To understand these things we must understand each part of the Bible in the context of the whole, and this means a firm

grasp of the Will of God which is the Gospel. A firm grasp of biblical priorities for our living will set us free from the contrary voices of our feelings, our culture, other people's expectations or Bible verses out of theological context. The grid which God has provided for our guidance is the Bible and we neglect it at our peril.[3]

Perhaps a better way of thinking about guidance would be in terms of our second diagram:[4]

Freedom and God's Moral Will

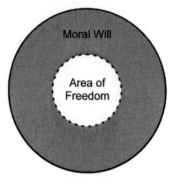

Here we acknowledge God's sovereign will; God working in and through all things to bring about his good purposes for his glory and his people's good, which includes using the decisions *we* make together with our prayers by weaving them into the tapestry of his plan. There is also God's moral will, doing what is right and avoiding what is wrong. But within that is an area of freedom. This is like the situation with Adam in the Bible, where he could name the animals in whatever way he saw fit and could not be 'out of God's will', that is, his moral will.

What is more, we are not to think that using our God-given reason, and maybe getting other people's advice so that in the end *we* make decisions, is somehow unspiritual. When you consider the New Testament apostles the language they often used was not that of 'discovering God's will for their lives' in terms of specific intention. Instead they use phrases such as: 'We thought it best' (1 Thess. 3:1); 'I think it necessary' (Phil. 2:25); 'If it seems advisable for me' (1 Cor. 16:4); 'I planned . . . to come to you' (Rom. 1:13), 'I hope to visit' (Rom. 15:24). Why? Because, the apostles were moving in the area of freedom in having desires and making plans, which no doubt they prayed about, some which came to fruition and others, like in Romans 1:13, which didn't, but they were evidently happy to rest secure in the knowledge that God was sovereign anyway.[5]

Decisions, decisions

There are basically three kinds of decisions we are often required to make.

First, there are right and wrong decisions. In the negative form you have the main ones in the Ten Commandments, not stealing, not murdering, not lying and so on. In the Sermon on the Mount Jesus intensifies these to include thoughts and motives as well as actions, being angry and unforgiving with someone in your heart for example (Matt. 5:21–22). Positively, Jesus sums up this aspect of God's will in terms of the two great commandments: Love the Lord your God with the whole of your being and love your neighbour as yourself (Mark 12:30–31). If we do that we won't go far wrong.

Secondly, there are wise/unwise decisions. Certainly we need wisdom to discern right from wrong and to negotiate our way through what is sometimes called the lesser of two evils (or in some cases the greater of the two goods). A classic example of this is given in the book which was made into a film called *The Cruel Sea*. It is the story of a captain of a British destroyer in the Atlantic during the Second World War who has to make an agonizing decision. The decision involves whether or not to drop depth charges into the sea because there is an enemy submarine which is attacking the convoy. The problem is that there are some British sailors in the water from a ship already sunk. If he fires the depth charges they will certainly die. But if he doesn't the chances are that there will be further sinkings and so more death because of the presence of the German submarine. What is he to do? Eventually, he decided to fire the depth charges which destroyed the submarine, but in so doing killed many of his own sailors too.

However, sometimes we are faced not with a matter of right or wrong but two apparently good options. For example, imagine that you have a young person about to go to university and there are two colleges with courses which are more or less the same, needing the same 'A' level grades. What do you do? Toss a coin perhaps? That is possible. But the person might want to ask some other questions such as these: is there a good Bible teaching church near one but not the other? Is there a Christian Union which would build me up and in which I could serve? Maybe there is a sick relative near one who would appreciate me visiting them. What is the wise thing to do? The important thing in making this kind of decision is asking questions which are Christ-centred rather than the self-centred, 'I will go to this university because of the prestige it will give me and increase the chances of getting a better paid job, even though there isn't much around in terms of gospel ministry.' That is not gospel-centred thinking.

Of course we need to avoid making foolish decisions.

Suppose we are invited out to a party which will end late on Saturday night. The Bible doesn't say much about the pros and cons of attending parties per se. It certainly does tell us that we must not get drunk or be a glutton. Other than that, attendance or non-attendance is a wisdom call. But we might want to factor into our thinking that if we are going to go to a late-night party, then we might not be in such a good state to attend God's word and serve his people on the following Sunday morning.

The Bible does not promise that God will protect us from making foolish or wrong decisions, and we will often have to live with the unpleasant consequences, but it does promise a way back to God when we do: 'No one whose hope is in you will ever be put to shame, but they will be put to shame who are treacherous without excuse' (Ps. 25:3). It is as we put our hope and trust in God through his Son that even the shame of some of the appalling bad decisions we make can be laid to rest, 'If we confess our sins, he is faithful and just and will forgive us our sins and cleanse us from all unrighteousness' (1 John 1:9).

In the third place there is what we can call 'who cares?' decisions. Some are so trivial that you have to ask whether it really matters. The Christian writer, Dr Jim Packer, relates the story of one Christian woman he knew who really did agonize and pray over which shoes to wear each day. But does it ultimately matter which shoes you buy or which meal you eat? The answer is: yes and no. 'No' in that if it is simply a choice between one pair of shoes and another or fruit salad over baked apple pie. But 'yes' if buying an expensive pair of shoes will get you into debt and use up money which would be better spent elsewhere. Or 'yes' if you are fostering a bad diet and so damaging your health. Then a 'who cares' decision becomes a 'wise/unwise' decision.

All of this brings us back to our fictional Adam and Eve story: what really matters has been revealed by God, namely, loving him with all our being and our neighbour as ourselves. If we are ever in doubt when making a decision, we are to bring these two commands into play to help out.

However, there is another 'will' which the great commandment points us to: God's saving will. How are we to love God with all our being and our neighbour as ourselves? By ourselves we can't. Also to love God with all we have, means embracing his call to believe:

Repent for the kingdom of heaven is near (Matt. 4:17).

Peter replied, 'Repent and be baptised, every one of you, in the name of Jesus Christ for the forgiveness of your sins. And you will receive the gift of the Holy Spirit. The promise is to you and your children and for all who are far off – for all whom the Lord our God will call (Acts 2:38–39.)

The Lord is not slow in keeping his promise, as some understand slowness. He is patient with you, not wanting anyone to perish but everyone to come to repentance (2 Pet. 3:9).

With all wisdom and understanding, he made known to us the mystery
of his will according to his good pleasure, which he purposed in Christ,
to be put into effect when the times reach their fulfilment – to bring
unity to all things in heaven and on earth under Christ. In him we were
also chosen, having been predestined according to the plan of him who
works out everything in conformity with the purpose of his will, in order
that we, who were the first to put our hope in Christ, might be for the
praise of his glory (Eph. 1:8–12, TNIV).

As Peter Adam writes, 'If we are to discuss Christians coming to
terms with God's Will then the central core of that Will is found in
Jesus Christ, his atoning death and resurrection, and the new lifestyle
that flows from God's work.'[6]

Objection!

Some, though, would raise the objection, 'What about the apostle
Paul in Acts 16 when he had a special dream from God to get him
to go to Macedonia?' There is no denying that happened but we
must remember that Paul was an *apostle* and this was a supernatural
event occurring at a significant turning point in the apostolic mission
with a moving of the gospel into Europe. In that sense it is special
and not normal. For every one supernatural work of guidance there
are dozens of non-supernatural wisdom guidance the apostles
engage in as we have seen. We are to be wary of making an exception
into a rule. But there are exceptions. And even in this case, Paul did
involve his colleagues to assess this guidance, 'After Paul had seen
the vision, we got ready at once to leave for Macedonia, concluding
that God had called us to preach the gospel to them' (Acts 16:10).

Some Christians talk about 'putting out a fleece' to find out God's
will. This is a reference to the story of Gideon in Judges 6. It is
usually thought of in terms of circumstantial signs, for example, 'If
I get a letter offering me that job before 3 pm next Tuesday I will
take it. If not I won't.' One could do that but it really wouldn't be

that much different from tossing a coin and saying 'heads I will take the job if offered and tails I won't'. In any case, most 'putting out of fleeces' has little to do with the story of Gideon. Gideon had been told by an *angel* what he was to do. That, I would imagine, would have sufficed for most of us, but not for him. He asked for *two* signs involving the fleece to substantiate what he had already been told: for the fleece to be dry in the morning when the surrounding ground was wet with dew and vice versa. These weren't circumstantial signs chosen at random ('If a white duck crosses my path on Thursday I will go to Bombay'), but *supernatural* events. More importantly, these were graciously given by God not as an example of guidance to follow but because Gideon was full of doubt and needed reassurance. In this regard we should *not* be like Gideon!

But what of the Holy Spirit, is he not involved? Of course! He is superintending all things to bring about God's sovereign will in the world, often unbeknown to us by keeping us from falling into holes of our own making. He was more than involved in inspiring the Scriptures to be written and is working in our minds to understand them and to move our wills to obey them. Furthermore, he is the Spirit of wisdom who, when we humble ourselves before him, will help us make wise choices and who in his sovereignty kindly clears up some of the mess we make when we are less than wise. The Holy Spirit is at work when God's word is preached and spoken by fellow Christians so I can glean their advice. He is at work in so many ways. Yes, *occasionally* there may be something very special and specific and unusual and I will thank him for that if it happens, but I won't get unduly upset if it doesn't. The promise is there in Psalm 25:9: 'He guides the humble in what is right and teaches them his way.'

It is liberating to know that while God sovereignly has a plan and purpose for my life, I don't have to worry trying to find out what it is. As Steven Roy rightly says,

> The partnership God seeks with us is not one of *determining* the course of my life but in *accomplishing* his purpose for my life . . . In the Lord's

prayer, Jesus taught us to pray that God's will would be done on earth (in our own lives first and foremost) as it is in heaven (Matthew 6:10). This petition has primary reference to God's revealed moral will, but I also believe it involves our willing submission to God's sovereign will. But God's will in both senses of the word, is something that already exists. Our partnership with him through prayer and active obedience in all the dimensions of life involves the carrying out of God's will, not determining what it will be.[7]

My task is to get on with being a Christian husband, father, grandfather, minister, brother, son and friend, where he has put me. I know his moral will pretty well, although I am sad to say I am not great at keeping it, but progress is slowly being made. I can rest in his sovereign will because nothing can mess that up. With God's help (which often means through the help of God's people), I can enjoy the wonderful freedom to make decisions which seem best to me at the time and relax, knowing that, 'All the ways of the LORD are loving and faithful for those who keep the commands of his covenant' (Ps. 25:10).

Let me conclude with some more wise words from Peter Adam:

> Ultimately our trust is not in a feeling of Guidance, an experience of Guidance, for that limits God to working through our feelings. Our trust in not in an experience of Guidance but in the God who guides, who upholds all things, who sustains the universe, who is accomplishing his good purpose to bring all things together under Christ, who calls us to know his will in the Gospel and his will is that we be made holy. Our call is to commit ourselves to this God and trust that he will guide us to his own glory.[8]

Questions for reflection and discussion

1. Make a list of the different ways that people think God guides us.

2. What kind of things do you ask God for guidance for? Should this change in any way in the light of God's providence and priorities for your life?

3. What steps would you take to try and make a 'wise' decision using the means God has provided?

4. If a friend comes to you with a difficult decision, how will you help them think about whether it is a right/wrong, wise/unwise, or a 'who cares' decision?

5. Think of some decisions you are seeking guidance on. How will the two principles of loving God with all our being and our neighbour as ourselves shape these decisions?

Notes

1. This parable is taken from Garry Friesen, *Decision Making and the Will of God* (Multnomah Press, 1980), p. 165–167.

2. Friesen, *Decision Making*, p. 178.

3. Peter Adam, *Guidance* (Grove Booklets, 1988), p. 13.

4. Friesen, *Decision Making*, p. 179.

5. Peter Adam criticises Friesen's approach to guidance (from which this diagram is taken) for denying that God has an individual will. The argument that is being maintained in this book however, is that God *does* have a specific will and purpose for the life of each individual (see the discussion on Ps. 139 and Joseph), but a trust in his sovereignty and a desire to humbly serve him means *we* do not need to know what this specific will is.

6. Adam, *Guidance*, p. 11.

7. Steven C. Roy, *How Much Does God Foreknow? A Comprehensive Biblical Study* (Apollos, 2006), pp. 256–257.

8. Adam, *Guidance*, p. 15.

8. PROVIDENCE AND SUFFERING (Job)

In the days before electronic surveillance, detective stories placed great store on information which could be gathered through keyholes. Without them what lay behind the doors would remain a mystery, but with them a glimpse of what was taking place in the room might be possible and with it the elimination of mystery, indeed, the solving of a crime.

However, as well as being useful, keyholes could be equally problematic. A handful of words heard without being able to be placed in their proper context might be quite misleading. What if there is someone in the room, a vital figure, who is just out of sight and earshot? Then our whole interpretation of an event could be seriously flawed.

This problem is captured by Kafka in *The Castle*. Minor servants become desperate after lifelong attempts to get beyond the impersonal outer circle of the castle's bureaucracy. To make up for their loss of dignity they fall back on a fantasy world where guesswork stands in for knowledge, where elaborate arguments are built on silences and conclusions drawn from a glance at raised eyebrows.

As the hero K says to Pepi, 'You chambermaids are used to spying through keyholes and from that you get this way of thinking, of drawing conclusions, as grand as they are false about a whole situation from some little thing you really see.'[1]

Herein lies the problem with keyholes. You don't always see enough to draw a firm conclusion, but once you have seen something, drawing a conclusion is very difficult to resist. This is the mistake of what Os Guinness labels 'keyhole theology'.[2] This limitation and temptation is especially important to bear in mind when we come to try to understand the relationship between providence and evil in God's world.

In earlier chapters we have been looking at what the Bible has to teach us about the reassuring doctrine of providence, 'God our heavenly Father working in and through all things by his wisdom and power for the good of his people and the glory of his name.' This covers the *whole* of our lives from the moment we are conceived to the moment we die. But what are we to make of what might be termed the 'shadow side of providence'? It is not difficult to imagine the response: 'Yes, I can see how, for example, a beautifully formed baby makes us marvel at God's providential work, but what about the abnormally formed baby? I can understand to some degree how God shapes our lives by the parents we have, but what of abusive parents?' While there is no easy answer to these sorts of questions (and the Bible's emphasis is not so much on us trying to fathom out why such things happen but to roll up our sleeves to help those to whom such things are happening), nonetheless it affirms quite strongly that even *these* things fall within God's providence.

One of the books in the Bible which helps us understand that God is still at work in the dark and perplexing times and underscores the limitations of our perspective – living *this* side of the keyhole – is the story of Job.

The book of Job is set out as a court case. So let us attend the assizes by imagining ourselves sitting in the public gallery to see how this drama unfolds and discover why bad things happen to good people. God is being tried.

The indictment

There are two viewpoints or perspectives we need to be aware of as we approach this story. First, there is the perspective of the various individuals in the drama. Secondly, there is the perspective of the book as *a whole*, which includes the unseen heavenly reality. This distinction is crucial, for the difference in perspective makes all the difference in the world for how we deal with the problem of suffering and evil. We may think of it in this way: the characters in the drama are looking through the keyhole and can only see a *part* of what is going on, but they tend to mistake it for the *whole* picture. However, as we the readers of the book are taken beyond the keyhole into the 'room' as it were, we begin to see that there is much more to what is happening than initially meets the eye.

In the book's first two chapters we are introduced to Job. He lives at a time when a person's wealth is measured not in terms of the size of someone's bank balance but the size of a person's herds. This would place him in the period of the Hebrew patriarchs, with men like Abraham, Isaac and Jacob. What is more, we are told that he lived in Uz, which would locate the story somewhere in the Arabian Desert. Unlike Abraham he is not given a family tree and so it would seem that he is being put forward as a representative of humanity as a whole and so may not be an Israelite.[3]

Job is not only a wealthy man; he is also a godly man. We are told that *'he feared God and shunned evil'* (1:1). His deep personal piety showed itself in several ways, not least in his passionate concern for the spiritual well-being of his children. In Job 1:4–5 we read that just in case his sons and daughters had behaved in ways that might have offended God and brought down his judgment upon them, Job went out of his way to make sacrifices for their sin on their behalf.

In order to pre-empt any cynical doubt which may be in our minds that all of this wealth has been gained by shady double-dealing, it is made quite clear from the outset that Job is 'blameless and upright' (1:8); in other words, his moral character was impeccable. Here, then, we have a sincere worshipper of God, an honest hard-working businessman, a loving husband and thoughtful father who is second to none; in fact Job almost appears to be too good to be true. But as we shall see, Job was one of those rare individuals which exist within a class all by themselves; he was a genuinely good man. Today we might describe Job as a committed Christian, one whose faith penetrated every area of his life. He is a model of what the Bible calls the 'wise man'.

So what could go wrong? This is when the scene switches to the unseen heavenly reality where an angelic being called 'Satan' comes into God's presence. The word 'Satan' here is not a proper name like 'Bill', rather it is a description of the angel's *role*; it is a word which means 'accuser' or 'prosecutor', we might even say, 'barrister'. What we are to note is that the angelic barrister does not accuse Job of doing anything wrong, except maybe having dubious motives for living a godly life; rather it is *God* who is being accused of setting up a phony arrangement amongst human beings by blessing righteous behaviour with rewards, and this, the Satan argues, hampers true righteousness. This is the first charge levelled against God in the book: 'Does Job fear God for nothing? . . . Have you not put a hedge around him and his household? You have blessed the work of his hands . . . but stretch out your hand and strike everything he has got and he will curse you' (1:9–11). 'The only reason why Job behaves as he does', argues the Satan, 'is because he knows on which side his bread is buttered. He is religious and moral only because of what he can get out of it. After all, everyone knows that religion is nothing but enlightened self-interest. It's just a matter of the right carrot and stick with Job. In fact, you can put it all down to his rather fortunate circumstances which *you* God, have provided. Anybody can afford to be religious when they have a lifestyle like that!' The underlying point he is making is that with this kind of arrangement one can never know whether people are being truly righteous for righteous-ness's sake or simply being good *in order* to enjoy blessings. In short, the Satan is charging God with setting up a flawed system. There is only one way to find out, he argues, and that is to put Job to the test. God is confident he will pass it and so he allows the Satan to do his worst. Well, perhaps not quite his worst, because God will not permit Job to be killed. Satan can go so far but no further; God still remains sovereign in setting limits.

The drama then begins to intensify; one moment all is calm, the next moment all is chaos.

The first thing to disintegrate is Job's financial empire: raiders attack his oxen, donkeys and camels, carrying them off and killing his servants. Then the fire of God falls from the sky and burns up the sheep and the servants (1:14–17). This is an economic disaster of epic proportions. But even that catastrophe is nothing compared to the devastating news which comes hard on its heels: Job's children were all in one house when a storm blew in and took them with it (1:18–19). Shell-shocked, Job looks out the window into the sky that seems to be getting darker by the minute. He no doubt is praying, hoping that things can't get any worse – when they do! He feels pain in his chest and his skin can't bear to be touched. Job's life is in utter ruins and so he crawls to the local rubbish tip to die:

> Why did I not perish at birth,
>   and die as I came from the womb?
> Why were there knees to receive me
>   and breasts that I might be nursed?
> For now I would be lying down in peace;
>   I would be asleep and at rest
> with kings and counsellors of the earth,
>   who built for themselves places now lying in ruins,
> with rulers who had gold,
>   who filled their houses with silver (3:11–15).

It is at this point that the second charge against God falls into place, which is the opposite of the first. As we shall see in a moment, most of the characters in the story have bought into the idea that God simply operates a rewards/retribution arrangement: good people get a good life while bad people get a bad life. That is what Job's three friends, Eliphaz, Bildad and Zophar argue. They see a strict cause-and-effect moral mechanism operating within God's universe similar to the law of gravity: what goes up must come down; good must be rewarded and bad punished. Occasionally, and con-troversially, some have suggested that children born with deformities are somehow being punished by God. That is the kind of idea that is in the foreground here. Job's case against his Maker is that God is being unjust to allow the righteous to suffer and that his system of rewards for good behaviour and punishment for bad simply isn't working for he, Job, *is* innocent.

The courtroom

This is not a literal courtroom, but the debate that is occurring and the way matters develop is the sort of thing that would have happened in an ancient Near Eastern court. Remember that every-one is buying into the retribution theory: good is rewarded and evil is punished and that is how God shows he is just – so they think. Three claims are being laid out: 1) God is just, 2) Job is righteous, and 3) the retribution principle is true. However, all three can't be right at the same time in *this* instance. At least one of them has to go for the tension to be relieved.

The way the next stage in the drama is set out is as follows: each of Job's friends in turn attacks him verbally. After each assault Job defends himself. This cycle of attack, defence and counter-attack is repeated three times, until eventually Job explodes in one long outburst, reducing his friends to silence. Even so, he still does not succeed in convincing them that he is innocent. Their minds were made up and they didn't want to be confused by the facts.

Job's three friends look at what is happening to Job and in effect say, 'Everyone knows God is just. What is more, everyone knows that suffering is punishment for wickedness. You are suffering terribly Job, and so the conclusion we are drawn to is that you must have done something *really* bad to deserve this. All you have to do is say sorry to God, appease him in some way and all will be well.' For his friends, it is *Job* who is in the dock and guilty. We see this in Eliphaz's speech in 4:7–9: 'Consider now: Who being innocent has ever perished? Where were the upright ever destroyed? As I have observed, those who plough evil and those who sow trouble reap it. At the breath of God they are destroyed.' The same line of attack is pursued later by Bildad:

> How long will you say such things?
>> Your words are a blustering wind.
> Does God pervert justice?
>> Does the Almighty pervert what is right? . . .
> Ask the former generations
>> and find out what their fathers learned,
> for we were born only yesterday and know nothing,
>> and our days on earth are but a shadow.
> Will they not instruct you and tell you?
>> Will they not bring forth words from their understanding?
>>> (8:2–3, 8–10).

However, for Job it is *God* who is in the dock, for in each case, he protests his innocence and challenges God to make his presence known so that Job can question him about the way he is running the world which, in his view, is not all that well. Job's reasoning can be put in the form of a syllogism, with major premise, minor premise and conclusion: Suffering is punishment for wickedness (major premise); Job is innocent (minor premise); therefore God must be unjust (conclusion):

> As surely as God lives, who has denied me justice,
>> the Almighty, who has made me taste bitterness of soul,
> as long as I have life within me,
>> the breath of God in my nostrils,
> my lips will not speak wickedness,
>> and my tongue will utter no deceit.
> I will never admit you are in the right;
>> till I die, I will not deny my integrity (27:2–5).

Elsewhere he cries,

> I loathe my very life;
>> therefore I will give free rein to my complaint
>> and speak out in the bitterness of my soul.
> I will say to God: Do not condemn me,
>> but tell me what charges you have against me.
> Does it please you to oppress me,
>> to spurn the work of your hands . . . ? (10:1–3)

Later on in the courtroom drama another much younger man comes onto the scene, an Israelite called Elihu who claims that they are all wrong (Job 32 – 37)! He is obviously an angry young man. He has not spoken because he feels that as a younger person it is both wise and respectful to allow his elders to have their say first. We see this in 32:6: 'I am young in years and you are old, that is why I was fearful, not daring to tell you what I know.' Eventually, however, he comes to the point where he can't contain his anger any longer. He has listened to the three counsellors and to Job, and in his view they are all to be found wanting. The three friends have simply not answered Job's objections, as Elihu points out in 32:12; Job has run rings around them until eventually they gave up trying to argue, being reduced to adopting the 'we are right and you are wrong and that's all there is to it' posture. But Job too has incensed Elihu, not because of his protested innocence per se, but because he is eager to clear his own reputation at the expense of God's reputation:

> But you have said in my hearing –
>> I heard the very words –
> 'I am pure and without sin;
>> I am clean and free from guilt.
> Yet God has found fault with me;
>> he considers me his enemy.
> He fastens my feet in shackles;
>> he keeps close watch on all my paths.'

> But I tell you, in this you are not right,
>> for God is greater than man. (33:8–12)

Similarly, in 34:12 we read: 'It is unthinkable that God would do wrong, that the Almighty would pervert justice.' In effect he is saying to Job, 'You may well be as innocent as you say, and it will not do for your three friends to bring that into question; but by the same token it is not acceptable for you to impugn God's goodness. You may not have sinned so grossly when you started but you are coming pretty close to it now. You are wrong.'

The first reason why Elihu rightly believes Job to be wrong is because 'God is greater than man' (33:12). Not simply that he is more powerful, but that his plans and purposes are on such a grand scale, far more complex and involved than our tiny minds can ever fully fathom. 'Your problem,' Elihu is arguing, 'is that you are viewing God as if he were simply man writ large, as if he were nothing but a capricious spiteful tyrant acting without reason. Just because *we* cannot immediately see what that reason is doesn't mean that there isn't one. God's timescale and concerns are much bigger than ours and we need to remember that.'

Secondly, following through this line of thought, Elihu suggests an altogether different perspective for understanding suffering. Instead of looking *back* for some sort of *cause* for suffering and asking, 'Is this suffering due to Job's sin or God's injustice (when in fact it is neither)?', Elihu suggests that it might be more helpful to look *forward* to try and identify a *purpose* in suffering. In other words, if God is good and wise (and the supremacy of wisdom is celebrated in ch. 28 with a song), what we need to ask is, what possible good could there be in him allowing suffering like this? The answer Elihu gives is that it is part of God's way of correcting us and preventing us from going off the rails entirely, as he puts it: 'to turn man from wrongdoing and keep him from pride, to preserve his soul from the pit' (33:17–18). In 33:19 he speaks of a man being 'chastened on a bed of pain'. Later he claims that God makes people '*listen* to correction' (36:10) and '*speaks* to them in their affliction' (36:15). Job has already complained that God has not spoken, but Elihu suggests he is speaking 'now one way, now another' (33:14), that is he is speaking to Job *through* suffering. Job's other friends insisted that God should primarily be thought of as a judge, whereas Elihu suggests that the controlling model should be that of a teacher ('Who is a *teacher* like him?', 36:22). In other words, it is too narrow a view to think of all suffering as retribution; may it not be that some suffering is God's instruction? Now we are getting very close to having some insight as to a purpose in *this* pain, for Elihu is not rebuked by God as are the other counsellors. Why? Because Elihu was pretty well near the mark in what he said.[4]

Of course we can respond to this kind of correction in two ways. We can be like sulky children, locking ourselves away in our room, building up resentment towards God for the way he is treating us, refusing to open the door in response to his knocking. God gives us that choice. Elihu warns Job that he is in danger of letting that happen to him: 'Beware of turning to evil, which you seem to prefer to affliction' (36:21). *Or* we can be like obedient children who, while expressing the hurt and the pain, nevertheless in the midst of difficulty will ask, 'Lord, what are you teaching me through this?'

There is, however, another vitally important dimension to the world of suffering, and that is the operation of a malevolent spiritual being. It has been suggested that the question which lies at the heart of the whole book, the problem which demands a resolution, is found in 9:24 with the rather ambiguous question: 'If it is not he [God], then who is it?'[5] As Job surveys not only the desolation in his own life, but some of the chaos which erupts in the natural order as well as social upheavals in society as a whole, Job asks this penetrating question which reveals the inner tension he is feeling, while at the same time reaching out towards a possible answer. As we have seen, Job has two pillars of belief which uphold the edifice of his faith. First, that God is sovereign over all, that nothing can thwart him or surprise him, and so he rightly asks 'If it is not *he*' who is in some way behind such things, then who else can it be? But then this brings into question the other pillar of his belief that God is good, for how can a good God have a hand in such things? This is the bulwark that is starting to crumble as he contemplates so much ruin in the world in chapter 9.

It would seem that Job wants to affirm the sovereignty of God without attributing to God evil, for it is unthinkable that the God who is the source and definition of all goodness should be the originator of evil, and so we have the other aspect of the ambiguous cry, 'If it is not he, then *who* is it?' Perhaps now Job is entertaining the possibility that there *is* some other force or personality at work in the world, another 'who', one who is malevolent and wicked. Not a second god, for there is only one God, no concession is made to dualism as in Zoroastrianism. So could it be that somehow God maintains both his sovereignty and goodness by allowing such a being to act while still achieving his righteous purposes, using this being as an instrument?[6] In some cases this would involve punishing a wayward world, as if God were to say, 'If you refuse to have me as your loving ruler then here is the alternative ruler.' But perhaps sometimes he becomes an instrument not to punish the wicked but to test the faithful and so becomes more like a fire to refine faith? We the readers know from the first two chapters that such a creature does exist, he is called the Satan, but although Job may be groping towards this idea, he doesn't quite grasp it, and so he continues to feel the inner anguish of wanting to hold on to the goodness of God in the face of wickedness and his feeling of injustice.

A further unmasking of this evil occurs in vivid pictorial form in chapter 41 with the creature called the Leviathan.[7] This figure when considered alongside other forms of biblical revelation of a supernatural being opposed to God can be identified as the devil. The question which chapter 41 raises is, what is God doing with this creature? One thing which becomes clear is that this creature does not lie outside God's sovereign rule. This comes out in the first eleven verses and the claim in verse 11 that '*Everything* under heaven belongs to me'. Yes there is a devil, but as Martin Luther would often remark; 'He is *God's* devil', that is, he does not have free rein. God will even use *him* to bring about his righteous purposes in the world.[8]

We may think of the courtroom in which this drama has been worked out as a triangle with different people occupying one of three corners:[9]

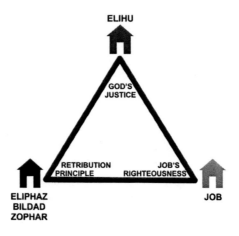

The trial

If God is in the dock, as he is in the minds of many people today like Christopher Hitchens, and in the mind of Job and the Satan, what must happen for him to lose his case? The quickest way would be for Job to take the advice of his wife, 'Curse God and die' (2:9), for then the Satan would have been right; Job was in the 'God business' only for what he could get out of it. This means that Job's 'righteousness' was nothing more than a disguised form of enlightened self-interest. It is sad to say that there are those who profess to be Christian believers who take that same attitude. They are only committed to their religion so long as they have a good job, good health, nice family and a thousand and one other things which make life pleasant. Dare God take away any of these, then he touches the apple of their eye and soon becomes an object of disdain. Of course, what they have been worshipping is a false god, a sugar-daddy god, who is no god at all. And maybe the sooner that is exposed the better.

The second way God could be vindicated is by Job following the advice of his friends in trying to appease God. Again this springs from a false view, that God is unprincipled and capricious like some drunken abusive father; you just never know when he is going to blow up so you are walking on eggshells all the time, forever anxiously trying to please him. But had Job gone along with this, the Satan's charge would have held, Job was only interested in himself and not truth or justice. Those are Satan's charges which don't stick, because Job doesn't give in; he really *is* righteous and God is vindicated in his choice of his man.

But what of *Job's* charge against God that he is being unjust? This would hold *if* the retribution principle were to remain unmodified. This is where the argument of Elihu comes into its own and is significant in that some hard things may come our way, not in order to punish us but to instruct us, perhaps getting us to change our priorities and checking our spiritual drift. It is obvious that the world doesn't operate in a strict cause-and-effect kind of way because we can see that many a good person has suffered terribly while many a tyrant has died peacefully in their sleep surrounded by a fortune (this is one of the major complaints of the psalmist in Ps. 73). So might it not be that things are a little more complicated in the world: bad things *do* happen to good people? But Job is still insistent that God appears and defends himself, and seems to take God's silence as a sign that he has surrendered to Job's accusations (31:35–37).

God eventually does appear and speaks but not quite as Job had hoped. 'Who is this that darkens my counsel with words without knowledge? Brace yourself like a man: I will question you, and you shall answer me' (38:2–3). It is Job who is put in the dock by God and it is he and not God who is required to answer a few questions:

> Where were you when I laid the earth's foundations? Tell me, if you understand. . . . Have you ever given orders to the morning, or shown the dawn its place . . . ? Have you entered the storehouses of the snow or seen the storehouses of the hail, which I reserve for times of trouble . . . ? Can

you bind the beautiful Pleiades? Can you loose the cords of Orion?
Can you bring forth the constellations in their seasons . . . ? (38:4–5, 12,
22, 31–32)

Job is barraged with question after question (38:39 – 39:30): 'What
about the animals? Do you provide for them, Job? Have you got so
great a mind that out of nothing you could come up with such a
strange looking bird as an ostrich? You think you are so wise,
Job, and I am so useless!' Job had wanted an interview with the
Almighty, and that is precisely what happened. It's as if God is
saying: 'Just who do you think you are Job? – God? To protest your
innocence is one thing, but to act so high and mighty that you accuse
me of injustice is another. In order to make the right judgment
upon me and what I am doing you have to have a lot more wisdom
and knowledge than you have. You have not been able to answer
any single one of my questions Job, questions to which I know all
the answers. Does it not therefore occur to you that I might, just
might, have the answer as to why I have permitted you to suffer? If
you cannot comprehend the intricacies of the creation which you
can see, then can you honestly expect to grasp all the mysteries of
suffering which you can't see? Only I, God, can do that.'

God's defence wasn't quite as Job expected. At the first pause Job
answers: 'I am unworthy – how can I reply to you? I put my hand
over my mouth' (40:4). The way litigation was carried out in an
ancient Jewish court was not for someone involved in a lawsuit to
convince the judge or jury of his innocence, but his accuser, so that
the plaintiff would withdraw his accusation and acknowledge defeat
by placing his hand over his mouth. That is what happened to Job,
his case against God collapsed like a stack of cards.

We might also ask: why should we presume that God owes us an
explanation as to why he allows suffering, any more than he owes
us an explanation as to why he made the ostrich the way he did? It
may be true that while *we* can't see why he should design so peculiar
a bird, no doubt God had plenty of good reasons for doing so, if
only known to himself, so could not the same be said for suffering?

More to the point, is it not reasonable to trust a God who has both the wisdom and the power to create so mind-boggling a universe, even if we may not be able to understand all the whys and wherefores of what happens in it?

Job finally realized his mistake, which is often ours, namely, to think that we are privy to *all* the facts, when we are not; we think we can see everything through the keyhole, but we can't. And our response should be that of Job's, not to rise up in arrogance and demand that God explain everything to us, but to repent of our presumption that we know better than God and fall down in worship.

> Then Job replied to the LORD:
> 'I know that you can do all things;
>> no plan of yours can be thwarted.
> You asked, "Who is this that obscures my counsel without knowledge?"
> Surely I spoke of things I did not understand,
>> things too wonderful for me to know.'
> You said, "Listen now, and I will speak;
>> I will question you,
>> and you shall answer me."
> My ears had heard of you
>> but now my eyes have seen you.
> Therefore I despise myself
>> and repent in dust and ashes.' (42:1–6)

Os Guinness writes:

> What was the root of Job's mistake in not suspending judgement? Was it his blasphemy? Not really. That was only the result. At the root of his problem lay a fallacy in his thinking (the notion that he had enough information to make proper judgements in such a situation). Once this fallacy was accepted, the blasphemy was an inevitable result. If this is so, it is curious to see that both Job and his friends made a very similar mistake . . . both Job and his friends press reason too far and make judgements where they have no right to.[10]

At the end of it all there are only two corners of the 'triangle' left. God *is* just and Job *is* righteous and the retribution principle is not true:

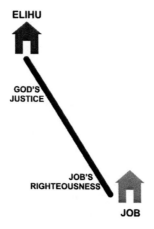

At the conclusion of the story we see something of God's grace being shown to Job in the way his former life is not simply restored but surpassed: 'After Job had prayed for his friends, the LORD made him prosperous again and gave him twice as much as before' (42:10).

It important that we don't see this simply as a form of 'compensation' for all that Job has suffered. Remember how right at the beginning it was the Satan's taunt that the only reason why Job was so religious was because of what he could get out of it, that there was some ulterior motive, namely, he was in it for what he could get? By taking everything away from Job, God demonstrated that the taunt had no real foundation. Even when he had nothing to entice him to believe in God, Job still trusted him. It wasn't a matter of Job thinking, 'Well, if I just hang on to the end there might be some goodies in store.' Job didn't know what the outcome was going to be; in fact it was more than likely he thought he was going to die. But nevertheless he trusted God.

But may this in fact be a pointer to heaven? We have to remember that this book of Job appeared early on in the history of Israel, before any clear ideas about heaven and the afterlife had been

revealed, although there is an inkling of the possibility of a future
life, as we see in chapter 19: 'I know that my Redeemer lives, and
that in the end he will stand upon the earth [lit. 'dust']. And after my
skin has been destroyed, yet in my flesh I will see God; I myself will
see him with my own eyes – I, and not another' (19:25–27). And so
just as it was only by God vindicating Job *in time* rather than at the
end of time that justice was seen to be done, so it is only by God
blessing Job *in this world* as well as in the next that it can be shown
that the righteous life is worth it after all.

However, we might still be tempted to object: 'But this is just a
story, real life isn't like that.'

A Christian couple whose life did echo that of Job was John and
Betty Stam. It was 6 December, 1934, Tsingteh, China. Betty was
bathing their three-month-old daughter when the Red Army surrounded the house. They took them captive and made them walk
to Miaosheo. There they bound John to a post for the night. The
next day they forced John and Betty to walk in their underwear
through the streets of the town and forced the people to come in
order to watch the execution. Outside town, in a clump of pine trees,
they beheaded John Stam with a sword while his wife watched. As
she fell over his body, they beheaded her. When the China Inland
Mission notified Betty's parents in Patterson, New Jersey, of the
death of their daughter and son-in-law, the mission received back a
telegram immediately: 'Deeply appreciate your consolation. Sacrifice
seems great, but not too great for Him who gave Himself for us.
Experiencing God's grace. Believe wholeheartedly Romans 8:28, "In
all things God works to the good for those who love him."' How
do we explain that? They were not unfeeling parents. However, they
were Christian parents. Not only they, but their other children knew
this to be true too. Betty's sister Helen wrote to her bereaved parents,

Dearest Daddy and Mother, you don't need to hear me say how much we
love you and are thinking of and praying for you in these days . . . I have
such radiant pictures of Betty and John standing with their palms of
victory before the Throne, singing a song of pure joy because they had

given everything they had to their Master, that I cannot break loose and cry about it as people expect. Crying seems to be too petty for a thing that was so manifestly in God's hands alone; but my heart is very, very sore for you.

Or in the words of Job, 'I *know* that my redeemer lives.'

Questions for reflection and discussion

1. What conclusions about God do people draw from the problem of suffering?
2. What had Eliphaz, Bildad and Zophar not understood about God's providence?
3. What can we learn from Elihu about how to counsel those who are suffering?
4. Are you tempted to look for the cause of suffering in your or other's lives? What problems are there with this?
5. How are we tempted to put God 'in the dock' in times of suffering? How does God's reply to Job (ch. 38 – 40) make you re-evaluate your attitudes in times of suffering?
6. If the doctrine of God's providence were not true, what would that mean for us in times of suffering?

Notes

1. Franz Kafka, *The Castle*, tr. Anthea Bell (Oxford University Press, 2009), p. 267.
2. Os Guinness, *Doubt: Faith in Two Minds* (Inter-Varsity Press, 1976), p. 197.
3. See Robert S. Fyall, *How Does God Treat His Friends?* (Christian Focus, 1995).
4. See Melvin Tinker, 'Purpose in Pain: Teleology and the Problem of Evil', *Themelios* 16.2 (1991), p. 15, <http://s3.amazonaws.com/tgc-documents/journal-issues/16.3_Tinker.pdf>.

5. Fyall, *How Does God Treat His Friends?*, pp. 62–73. See also Robert S. Fyall, *Now My Eyes Have Seen You: Images of Creation and Evil in the Book of Job* (Apollos, 2002).

6. This is a crucial element in moving towards an understanding of how God is sovereign over all things – including evil acts – without himself being the author of evil: 'How does God know of the causes of evil actions if he himself is not the cause of them? Augustine's answer is that God foreknows future evil by knowingly and willingly permitting particular evils to occur. For God to permit some event to occur does not entail that he brings that event about, but it is consistent with his foreknowledge of such events. God does not and cannot will evil actions, but he may nevertheless know that they will occur and be willing for them to occur. In permitting evil in this way God acts for the highest and holiest of reasons even though the detail of such reasons may be at present hidden from us' (Paul Helm, 'The Augustinian-Calvinist View', in James K. Beilby and Paul R. Eddy (eds.), *Divine Foreknowledge – Four Views* [InterVarsity Press, 2001], p. 176).

7. See Melvin Tinker, 'Evil Unmasked', <http://www.bethinking.org/suffering/introductory/evil-unmasked-Job-41.htm>.

8. One of the early church leaders who devoted a great deal of thought to the doctrine of providence was John Chrysostom (349–407). His greatest work on the subject, *Providence*, was written during a painful exile towards the end of his life. Chrysostom drew together the didactic (instructive) and adversarial (satanic) roles in God's purposes through providence. And so the healing of the paralytic by Jesus is taken as a 'sign of his greatest care for his welfare': 'For as a gold refiner having cast a piece of gold into the furnace allows it to be proved by the fire until such a time as he sees it has become purer: even so God permits the souls of men to be tested by troubles until they become pure and transparent and have reaped much profit from this process of sifting; wherefore this is the greatest species of benefit.' With regard to the work of Satan, this is seen as a means used by God to develop and mature the character of believers and so magnify the ministry of the gospel in the world: 'Nevertheless, though the devil had set so many traps, not only did he not shake the church, but instead made her more

brilliant. For during the period when she was not troubled she did not teach the world as effectively as she now does to be patient, to practise self-restraint, to bear trials, to demonstrate steadfast endurance, to scorn the things of the present life, to pay no regards to riches, to laugh at honor, to pay no heed to death, to think lightly of life, to abandon homeland, households, friends, and close relations, to be prepared for all kinds of wounds, to throw oneself against the swords, to consider all the illustrious things of the present life – I am speaking of honor, glories, power and luxury – as more fragile than the flowers of springtime.' Cited in Christopher A. Hall, *Learning Theology with the Church Fathers* (InterVarsity Press, 2002), pp. 183-205.

9. See John Walton and Andrew Hill, *Old Testament Today* (Zondervan, 2004), p. 307.

10. Guinness, *Doubt*, p. 208.

9. PROVIDENCE AND CONVERSION
(Acts 8:26–40)

What would you say is the greatest gift that God in his providence could ever bestow upon a person? Remember that we defined providence as, 'God our heavenly Father working in and through all things by his wisdom and power for the good of his people and the glory of his name.' Is it good health, a sound mind and a happy well-integrated family perhaps? These and many other things are to be received as gifts of God distributed through providence not only to believers but unbelievers as well. As Jesus said, 'He causes the sun to rise on the evil and the good, and sends rain on the righteous and the unrighteous alike' (Matt. 5:45). After all, that is the kind of God he is, overwhelmingly generous.

But for the Christian at least, the greatest fact which testifies to the sheer wonder and power of providence is that they are Christians at all. And so the seventeenth-century Puritan preacher, John Flavel writes:

> In nothing does providence shine forth more gloriously in this world
> than in ordering the occasions, instruments and means of conversion of
> the people of God. However skilfully its hand had moulded your
> bodies, however tenderly it had preserved them and how bountifully it
> had provided for them; if it had not ordered some means or other for
> your conversion, all the former favours and benefits it had done for you
> had meant little.[1]

If a dozen Christians were brought together at random, each one
would have a different story to tell of how God brought them to
himself. As has often been said, while there is only one way to God
there are many ways to Christ. For some this would have been a
matter of being brought up in a Christian home, with the result that
they can't remember a time when they did not have a personal faith
in Christ. For others it will have been through the faithful work of a
Sunday school that they gradually came to an awareness of their need
for a Saviour and that need being met by Christ. For others still, it
will have been in later years as a student or in mid-life or even older,
that the first steps towards discipleship were taken. In whichever of
these categories we find ourselves, the doctrine of providence will
lead us to the belief that God in his love, wisdom and power has so
ordered *all* events and people to bring Christians to the point when
they would experience his saving love. How else could it have been?
If he had set his heart upon us from all eternity, as Paul says ('Those
God foreknew he also predestined to be conformed to the likeness
of his Son', Rom. 8:29), that means he had to be intimately involved
in every minute detail of the *world's* history in order to shape our
personal history so that we would come to know him.

There is one episode in the Bible which perfectly illustrates this
astonishing truth: the story of Philip and the Ethiopian eunuch in
Acts 8.

In order to illustrate this aspect of God's providence I will share
how I see God's providential hand being at work in my life, so that
someone like me, who for many years wanted nothing to do with
Christ, was eventually found by him.

The lengths to which God goes

> Those who had been scattered preached the word wherever they went.
> Philip went down to a city in Samaria and proclaimed the Christ there.
> When the crowds heard Philip and saw the miraculous signs he did, they
> all paid close attention to what he said. With shrieks, evil spirits came out
> of many, and many paralytics and cripples were healed. So there was
> great joy in that city . . . Now an angel of the Lord said to Philip, 'Go
> south to the road – the desert road – that goes down from Jerusalem to
> Gaza.' So he started out, and on his way he met an Ethiopian eunuch, an
> important official in charge of all the treasury of Candace, queen of the
> Ethiopians (Acts 8:4–8, 26–27).

This is really quite remarkable. Philip is in Samaria at the vanguard
of what appears to be wholesale revival involving large-scale con-
versions and healings. This is clearly all part of God's plan as declared
by the Lord Jesus in Acts 1 when, before he ascended into heaven,
he gave the disciples their marching orders: 'But you will receive
power when the Holy Spirit comes on you; and you will be my
witnesses in Jerusalem, and in all Judea and Samaria, and to the ends
of the earth' (1:8). The gospel has already been proclaimed in
Jerusalem and Judea and here we are in the next critical stage of its
outward movement: Samaria. We are to notice the Samaritans were
paying close attention to what Philip had to say; folk were responding with great joy, reflecting on earth the joy in heaven (Luke 15:7,
10). Since things were going so well we might think that the divine
strategy would have been to keep Philip there as long as possible
(even Peter and John had turned up to see what was going on and
gave it their blessing, 4:14–17, 25). But God has another plan which
no-one would have entertained from a purely human point of view.
Indeed, it is so counterintuitive that God had to send an angel to
convince Philip that it was the right thing to do. The divine plan is
for Philip to leave the crowds, vacate the city and stand in the middle
of a desert road! That is not the place we would normally think of
going to in order do a spot of evangelism. It is hardly the place

where you will get a good hearing, apart from one or two vultures perched on a cactus! But Philip dutifully obeys and lo and behold, what does he see coming down the road but the equivalent of a six-door limousine, a royal chariot containing a top civil servant of a significant country. Why does God go to such lengths of taking Philip out of a vibrant mission field, ensuring that he and the Ethiopian just 'happen' to meet so precisely? It is because God wants *this* person to hear the gospel.

God wasn't making any mistakes at this point. He hadn't made a mess of the divine timetable. There was no clash of appointments such that he meant to have Philip in Gaza but he had overlooked that fact and had him in Samaria instead. No, while *we* may make such mistakes because of what we call unforeseen circumstances, God has no such limitations, he foresees everything. That, in part, is what it means to be God.

A moment's reflection reveals that Philip is a brilliant choice for this task. In the first place he has proved that he has been given the gift of an evangelist, that special unction of the Holy Spirit which enables him to lead people to faith. In the second place he has already been evangelizing folk who are beyond the pale as far as the Jews were concerned, for 'Jews do not associate with Samaritans' (John 4:9). In other words, he is a cross-cultural missionary of the first order who is not hung up by social barriers or religious prejudice (a lesson Peter still had yet to learn with Cornelius, see Acts 10). This means that he would be well disposed to speaking to a Gentile from Ethiopia, a eunuch at that, who under Old Testament law would not have been allowed to worship God in the temple. Philip is exactly the kind of person needed to share the gospel of God's saving love to such a rank outsider.

We then have the Ethiopian official himself. Luke describes him in verse 27 as an '*important* official in charge of all the treasury of Candice, Queen of the Ethiopians'. Someone like that is going to have tremendous influence back in his native country. This is someone who has the ear of the Queen. Therefore what he says will carry a lot of weight. Just think how many doors would be flung wide open for the gospel back in Ethiopia if this man gets converted. Indeed, the present Ethiopian Orthodox Church claims to have been founded by him.

I was raised with no Christian background at all, quite the contrary. Hailing from a strong coal-mining family, from a very early age I was steeped in socialist-communist principles which I took with me into my teenage years. Karl Marx's line that 'religion is the opiate of the people' seemed an accurate description of the church as far as I could see. So how was God going to bring someone like me, who wouldn't be seen dead going into a church or clutching a hymn book, to the position of giving Christianity a fair hearing? Strangely he began to do it through an informal game of football. One day during the summer holidays after I had completed my 'O' levels at the age of sixteen, I found myself bored with little to do, and so I thought that I would call on someone I had just got to know at school who lived in the next village. I turned up on his doorstep and together with a few friends of his we lumbered over to the local school playing field to kick a ball around. Later I went to his home to meet his parents and a friendship was struck up. Unbeknown to me at the time, this family was Christian, the first Christians, who to my knowledge, I had ever met. That is providence, seemingly insignificant things like a teenager's boredom, a casual acquaintance at school, and a knockabout game of football God superintends and uses to gain the attention of an awkward unbelieving teenager.

The extent to which God prepares

This man had gone to Jerusalem to worship, and on his way home was sitting in his chariot reading the book of Isaiah the prophet. The Spirit told Philip, 'Go to that chariot and stay near it.'

Then Philip ran up to the chariot and heard the man reading Isaiah the prophet. 'Do you understand what you are reading?' Philip asked. 'How can I,' he said, 'unless someone explains it to me?' So he invited Philip to come up and sit with him.

The eunuch was reading this passage of Scripture:

'He was led like a sheep to the slaughter,
    and as a lamb before the shearer is silent,
    so he did not open his mouth.
In his humiliation he was deprived of justice.
    Who can speak of his descendants?
    For his life was taken from the earth.'

The eunuch asked Philip, 'Tell me, please, who is the prophet talking about, himself or someone else?' Then Philip began with that very passage of Scripture and told him the good news about Jesus (Acts 8:27–35).

It is hardly ever the case that someone becomes a Christian believer totally 'out of the blue', overnight. There is usually God providentially doing some groundwork long before so that the seed of the gospel will find receptive soil. That is clearly the case here. To begin with, the Ethiopian would be what today might be referred to as a 'warm contact', since we are told that he 'had gone to Jerusalem to worship'. He wasn't a Jew, nor was he a Samaritan. He was not even what is called a 'proselyte' or a convert to Judaism. However, he was someone who was interested in the religion of Israel, hence him coming back from Jerusalem reading part of the Old Testament Scriptures. He is an example of a Gentile 'God-fearer'. These were people who were unwilling or unable to submit to the ceremony of circumcision and so they worshipped God from afar. Somehow God had brought this man under the sound of the Old Testament, maybe through his official visits to Israel. As a result he had some sort of framework, together with the necessary categories, which would help him understand the gospel when it was eventually explained to him. This means he would have known that there is but one God who is Creator of all. This truth would have been coupled with the belief that he was holy and human beings are cut off from him by their sin. From the Old Testament Scriptures he would have been aware that God had taken steps to provide sacrifices, limited though they were, to enable people to draw close to him. He would have been alerted to God's promise to establish a king on David's throne for ever (2 Sam. 7), a Messiah to establish his reign on earth. That is a fair amount of basic knowledge for someone to have which would have been invaluable to an evangelist like Philip.

But remarkably God had been overruling in another way which borders on the miraculous, for God superintended events so that the Ethiopian would be reading a *certain passage* of the Old Testament when Philip came along, part of Isaiah 53: 'He was led like a sheep to the slaughter and as a lamb before the shearer is silent, so he did not open his mouth.' Not only is this a gift of a text for anyone wanting to explain the person and work of Jesus Christ, but it is what lies on the other side of it that is particularly interesting. We have to realize that he was not reading a book, but a scroll, and scrolls came in sections. Why would the Ethiopian be reading *this* section rather than any other? This, it has to be admitted is conjecture, but it could be because of what came next in Isaiah, 'Let not any eunuch complain, "I am only a dry tree" . . . To the eunuchs who . . . hold fast to my covenant – to them I will give within my temple and its walls a memorial and a name better than sons and daughters' (Is. 56:3–5). This is a promise that when the Christ comes eunuchs will no longer be banned from being part of the people of God (Deut. 23:1). That would have meant a lot to this man. He admired the Jewish religion and maybe he wanted to be part of it, but he couldn't, his physical state excluded him. Yet here is a promise that one day that will all change. Many of us often turn to our favourite passages of the Bible time after time, thinking of those promises which mean so much to us. Here is God's providence at work in the detail in that the Ethiopian couldn't purchase this part of the scroll without purchasing Isaiah 53. This means that the man's sad state of being a eunuch is not lost on God. Do we not think that in eternity God didn't specifically have *this* man in mind when he inspired Isaiah to write this particular portion of Scripture? It wasn't *just* for him of course but it *was* for him. God is that great, weaving *everything* together so that people can be saved.

However, having the Bible is one thing, understanding it is another. Accordingly, God providentially prepares Bible teachers and evangelists like Philip so that he can use them to bring the message of his saving love to folk like this man. In a million and one ways God has been at work years before, even centuries before, so that this divine encounter could take place. He does that with all those he wants to reach out to with the gospel.

Philip then explains the passage to him, that this prophecy has been fulfilled in the God-man from Nazareth, the Lord Jesus Christ. He is the one led like a lamb to the slaughter on a cross, who died to put away the sins of all those who put their trust in him as a sacrifice and was raised from the dead to 'justify many'. Philip had personally met the apostles who could testify to all of this.

I take it that it was within the providence of God that I was born into a country where Christians can freely tell other people about the Lord Jesus Christ. I was also brought up at a time when religious education was taught in schools and the set form of worship was essentially Christian. This meant that although I didn't know what the Christian message was (as it was never properly explained to me at school), I knew much of the Bible's basic content, including the life of Jesus, the stories of his death and resurrection and the early spread of Christianity. We were also given free Bibles, courtesy of the Gideon Society, and all of this was instrumental in preparing me for the time when the Christian message would not only be explained to me, but displayed to me by a family who really did know God and love him. This is the experience of most Christians. In countless ways God has made it possible for them to hear him speak; making his overtures of love to them.

A response which God requires

As they travelled along the road, they came to some water and the eunuch said, 'Look, here is water. Why shouldn't I be baptized?' And he gave orders to stop the chariot. Then both Philip and the eunuch went down into the water and Philip baptized him. When they came up out of the water, the Spirit of the Lord suddenly took Philip away, and the eunuch did not see him again, but went on his way rejoicing (Acts 8:36–39).

God has given us his book, together with people to explain it, not simply to provide us with information but to bring about a transformation. This is what Jesus calls being 'born again', a change on the inside whereby God becomes a living reality, leading to changes on the outside which show as we begin to live out that reality. Baptism is a sign of that taking place or a promise by God to make it true. The Ethiopian had obviously followed Philip's logic through that if we believe Jesus is God's promised Son, who is to be in charge of our lives, and baptism is a sign of obeying the gospel and water is available, then you get on with the business – get baptized now! We are not to be slow or lazy in responding to God's providential overtures.

At the beginning of August 2010 I received a letter from the father of the family through whom I became a Christian. He is now in his late eighties and had recently read a book I had just written. This is part of what he wrote:

As I was reading your book my mind was time and time again drawn to William Cowper's wonderful hymn, 'God moves in mysterious ways . . . ' My mind also went back to a day in 1971 when I came home from work and asked Lois [his wife] 'What sort of day have you had?' Tea was delayed as I heard how a young 16 year old had spent the afternoon talking about the future. Melvin was concerned about whether he would be able to go to university or not. I gathered that the conversation went on for about 2 hours. Lois let it be known that he would always be welcome at our home and suggested he have a big talk with his Dad and Mam. A few days later we were delighted to know that university was to be the way forward. The visits became more regular and invitations to attend Sunday services were accepted. The rest is history, for the Lord opened your heart Melvin, as the Holy Spirit spoke to you through the Word and you could sing and mean, 'O happy day that fixed my choice on Thee my saviour and my God.' Praise the Lord.

My 'parent in Christ' uses some telling phrases in describing my conversion. He speaks of the Lord 'opening my heart' and the Holy Spirit, 'speaking through the Word'. These underscore the primacy of God in conversion as in all his providential works. Although this is a massive topic in its own right, it might be worth very briefly exploring this particular aspect of providence.

Sometimes this drawing of God to himself by the Holy Spirit through the gospel message is referred to as 'irresistible grace'. What this entails can be illustrated by the story I once heard Dr J. I. Packer tell of something which happened to him.[2]

He related how, when he was a student at Oxford University, he had gone punting on the river and had fallen head first into the River Thames. He said it was a dreadful experience; the water was cold, murky and deep. What is more, his arms and legs had become entangled in a mass of thick weeds. For a while he thought he was finished. He then imagined what his fellow students who were still in the punt might have said.

One could have called out: 'You will be all right. You can get out of the water if you want to. Just keep on struggling and eventually you will make it.' A second might have said: 'I would like to help you, but I do have a problem with my conscience for I don't want to interfere with your free will. But I can give you some tips about swimming if you like.'

Those two imagined reactions parallel two views of how we obtain salvation in Christ which have appeared in different guises throughout the history of the church. One is called Pelagianism, the other Arminianism. Both believe that the work of Jesus upon the cross is vitally important and central for our salvation. But both believe that for that work to become effective in our lives we have to make a contribution of our own. Christ's death is necessary but not wholly sufficient to ensure our personal salvation. What is also necessary is our own self-generated faith; whereas the apostle Paul insists that this itself is a gift of God as it is not natural to us (Eph. 2:8).[3]

The Pelagian believes that we all have a natural ability to believe if we want to; our fallen nature, what the Bible calls 'the flesh' *(sarx)*, is not a barrier. Indeed, it is within our nature to believe as a matter of the will.

Arminianism is a little different in that it readily agrees that supernatural help is required for us to believe the gospel (the 'work of the Holy Spirit speaking through his Word'), but this is open to everyone and can be resisted if we so choose.

In both cases God is dependent upon us *choosing* to respond to him. In one way or another both amount to saying: 'If you want to be saved you have to make the final step, God can only go so far, you have to do the rest.' But what if our spiritual state is akin to the physical state Dr Packer found himself in, drowning, and self-effort isn't enough?

Dr Packer developed the illustration further. When he fell into the river, he was immensely glad that the people in the punt were neither Pelagian nor Arminian, but Calvinists (those who uphold the sovereign providence of God covering all things). What actually happened was that a friend of his jumped into the river, overcame his hapless struggles, pulled him free of the reeds, brought him back to the shore, gave him artificial resuscitation and revived him. 'That,' said Dr Packer, 'is what I call a rescue!'

Luke, who wrote the book of Acts, uses precisely this kind of language to describe conversion in the case of Lydia: 'The Lord opened her heart to respond to Paul's message' (Acts 16:14). Sometimes we speak of ourselves 'opening our heart to Jesus' and that certainly is the way it feels, and from one point of view that is an entirely accurate description. But in terms of the *initiative and primary work of salvation,* it is right to stress that it is the Lord who opens hearts. As he opens our hearts by way of the gospel, we are truly freed to open our hearts to that gospel.

All of this is a piece with the view of providence that we have been exploring, the great and gracious God working in and through all things for his glory and our good. If it is true as John Flavel writes, 'In nothing does providence shine forth more gloriously in this world than in ordering the occasions, instruments and means of conversion of the people of God', then it is not possible to believe that at the most crucial stage of our lives, entering into a personal, saving relationship with God through his Son, that God steps back to create a 'space' for the unknown: will we or won't we respond to his gracious overtures in the gospel? It is difficult to believe such a thing for at least two reasons.

First, if God has been at work in the seemingly 'insignificant' events in our lives to bring us to this point, it would be inconsistent (to say the least) that at the most significant point he decides to 'let go'. Indeed, it is especially in conversion that the compatibilist position sees God's sovereignty and human responsibility coming together harmoniously. In fact, it is a strong belief in God's sovereignty that gives the evangelist confidence to speak into what would otherwise be a futile situation (given a human being's natural disposition regarding the things of God, Eph. 2:1).[4]

In the second place, the text which has provided the melodic line for this book, Romans 8:28, is only part of a rich tapestry of verses which tie together God's electing grace in salvation and its climax in glory which includes God's sovereign work in calling a person to faith:

> And we know that in all things God works for the good of those who love him, who have been called according to his purpose. For those God foreknew he also predestined to be conformed to the image of his Son, that he might be the firstborn among many brothers. And those he predestined, he also called; those he called, he also justified; those he justified, he also glorified (Rom. 8:28–30).

On this John Piper writes:

> Therefore what this magnificent text (Romans 8:28–30) teaches is that God really accomplishes the complete redemption of his people from start to finish. He foreknows (elects) a people for himself before the foundation of the world, he predestines his people to be conformed to the image of his Son, he calls them to himself in faith, he justifies them through that faith, and he finally glorifies them. And nothing can separate them from the love of God in Christ forever and ever (Romans 8:39).[5]

In other words, election, calling to faith through the gospel, sanctification and glorification form a seamless continuity, held together by the personal, sovereign work of God. The result is that it is then God who receives all the glory:

> Oh, the depth of the riches of the wisdom and knowledge of God!
>> How unsearchable his judgments,
>> and his paths beyond tracing out!
> 'Who has known the mind of the Lord?
>> Or who has been his counsellor?'
> 'Who has ever given to God,
>> that God should repay them?'
> For from him and through him and for him are all things.
>> To him be the glory forever! Amen (Rom 11:33–36).

Questions for reflection and discussion

1. Reflecting on the story of Philip and the Ethiopian (Acts 8), try to make a list of everything that comes together by God's providence.
2. Think about your own story of being saved; how had God been preparing you to receive the gospel? What can you see of God's providence in your actually hearing the gospel?
3. Why is it important to acknowledge God's total sovereign providence in your conversion, including the final step?
4. In what ways does God's sovereign providence affect your own efforts to share the gospel?

Notes

1. John Flavel, *The Mystery of Providence* (Banner of Truth Trust, 1991), p. 60.
2. The author heard this as a student.

3. 'On an incompatibilist view of freedom, God's grace can only ever be
    causally necessary, not causally sufficient, for the production of faith . . .
    Divine grace and such a choice are then together causally sufficient for
    faith in Christ, for the personal appropriation of Christ . . . With such
    freedom, God's saving grace is always resistible, and so saving grace can
    never ensure its intended effect' (Paul Helm, 'The Augustinian-Calvinist
    View', in James K. Beilby and Paul R. Eddy (eds.), *Divine Foreknowledge
    – Four Views* [InterVarsity Press, 2001], p. 170).
4. See J. I. Packer, *Evangelism and the Sovereignty of God* (Inter-Varsity Press,
    1961), pp. 106–121.
5. John Piper, *The Pleasures of God* (Multnomah Press, 1991), p. 141.

10. PROVIDENCE – HARD AND HOPEFUL
(Ruth)

It was one of the most disturbing and poignant snapshots of the Vietnam War: a little girl running naked down the street, screaming in pain, her eyes squeezed tight with terror. Many believe it was a picture which helped America lose that war.

Twenty-four years later, in 1996, Americans saw another picture of the same girl, now a young woman, poised by the Vietnam Veterans' Memorial in Washington DC. It was Veterans' Day. As a child Kim Phuc brought home to Americans the horror of war, today she teaches quite a different lesson, the healing power of forgiveness.

As she laid the wreath at the wall, Kim told the assembled crowd of war veterans, 'As you know, I am the little girl who was running to escape from the napalm fire. I have suffered a lot from both physical and emotional pain. Sometimes I thought I could not live, but God saved my life and gave me faith and hope.'

Soon after that infamous photo was taken, Kim was rushed to a hospital by the Associated Press photographer who had taken it.

Years of painful burn therapy followed. After the war she enrolled
at Saigon university hoping to become a doctor, but she was far too
valuable a propaganda tool for the communists and so she was put
to work as a government secretary. In 1986 she was sent to Cuba on
a goodwill visit, where she met and married a Christian, Bui Huy
Toan. Kim too had become a believer. They both managed to defect
and more recently on national radio they told of their plans to go
to Bible college and then to spread the gospel amongst the
Vietnamese people. As Kim shared the meaning of forgiveness to
thousands of toughened soldiers on that Veterans Day ceremony,
she publicly forgave the unknown pilot whose load had scared her
skin and killed her two younger brothers. At that moment, many of
these hardened veterans simply began to weep.

What is the moral of that story? It is this: there is no limit to
God's restoring love. From what many would have considered to
be a hopeless situation and an insignificant girl, God began to restore
a nation. On that bleak day when Kim lost her family and was
engulfed in flames, she would not have been able to envisage in
a million years the unlikely outcome of her ordeal, that through a
series of apparently 'chance' events, she would come to know the
healing power of God's love and in turn share that love with
thousands of others, as she is still doing today. Through her
testimony many have discovered for themselves the peace that can
be had under the divine 'wings of refuge'.

This is, in fact, the burden of the book of Ruth. As such it forms
a fitting conclusion to our study as it draws together many of the
strands regarding the doctrine of providence we have been looking
at: God working universally and specifically superintending all the
details of life, the hard times and the good, the short-term and
the long-term, in order to bring about his good and loving purposes
in a world which has turned its back on him. For the characters in
the drama, many of God's actions are opaque and mysterious,
drawing from them simple, obedient faith.

One of the most striking things about this story is that it is so
ordinary, dealing with everyday events: economic hardship, death,

love, marriage, birth. What is more, the people are so ordinary too. Ruth has no strange visions of God, she hears no prophetic voice and never sees a miracle. Neither do the people around her. It is all very humdrum and mundane. And yet it is in and through the ordinary day-to-day things of life and the most unassuming of people that God is mightily at work, moving secretly and silently to bring about his great plan of salvation for the world. Of course the same is true today. We are not to make the mistake of thinking that God is only to be found in the impressive and spectacular. He is also to be found in the ordinary and seemingly trivial. It is not just with the great spiritual superheroes he is concerned, people like Gideon, but those who appear to be the most ordinary of people simply seeking to love him and serve him the best they can, people like Ruth.

Two historical references lie either side of the main narrative and their significance should not be overlooked. The first reference is in 1:1, 'In the days when the judges ruled there was a famine in the land'. The other is at the end in 4:22 and the concluding genealogy, 'Obed the father of Jesse, and Jesse the father of *David*'. The question which comes to mind is this: how do we get from the situation of the days of the judges when 'Israel had no king; everyone did as he saw fit' (Judg. 21:25) to the situation when there was God's king on the throne in the person of David? This is the story which in part tells us how, and it is a sublime masterpiece of providence.

So let us trace out the path of providence in this story, high-lighting the main features.

Hard providence

'It was the best of times, and the worst of times', so begins Charles Dickens's, *A Tale of Two Cities*. This tale of two women could have begun like that too, although it was veering towards one of the worst of times. We are told that we are in the period of the 'Judges',

a time of moral and spiritual decline, only arrested by God's inter-
mittent intervention in the raising up of a 'judge' or 'rescuer' like
Samson.

In chapter 1, the family of Elimelech is Israel in microcosm, a
people on the run from God. There is a famine in the land, probably
caused by war but also forming part of God's chastening judgment
(Deut. 32:24). As a result, Elimelech and his family decide to leave
Bethlehem, a name which means 'house of bread', which is now a
house of famine, and move to Moab. It is important for us to grasp
the seriousness of this action.

To leave the land of promise was tantamount to leaving the faith.
It was a turning one's back on God himself. And if that were not
bad enough, going to a place like Moab made matters worse. For
these were the sworn enemies of God's people, folk steeped in
idolatry. Indeed, God had expressly forbid his people to have any
dealings with them (Deut. 23:3–6). What this family was doing was
the cultural equivalent of a professing Christian walking away from
church or tearing up their baptism certificate with the exclamation,
'From now I am going to throw in my lot with the Jehovah's
Witnesses.' Why should this be so? After all, on the surface it seems
that it was simply a matter of expediency; there is a famine, so why
not go to where there is food? It is meant to be a temporary arrangement after all (Ruth 1:1). However, there are several clues in the
passage which indicate that there was more to it than that.

One clue is the names of the characters which the writer seems
to stress. Take, for example, the name Elimelech. It means 'my God
is king'. There is irony there. As one of God's people, he was meant
to trust God come rain or shine. But despite his name, he was no
better than anyone else in Israel, for he too simply did what was
right in his own eyes. His name claimed one thing, 'God is my king',
his actions revealed something else, 'I am my own king'. Also, he
was an Ephrathite belonging to a well-established, even wealthy,
family. This is hinted at by Naomi in 1:21 where she says that she
went away 'full' but came back 'empty'. Material comfort then, rather
than spiritual faithfulness was at the top of this family's agenda. The

names of his sons may be significant too. They are prophetic names pointing to what happens when we deliberately turn our backs on God; we become Mahlon (which means 'sickly') and Kilion ('failing'). Also, they are Canaanite names, and so religious compromise might have been there from the start. The result was disaster, for all the men died, and we read, 'Naomi was left without her two sons and her husband' (1:5). Do you not detect the pathos? What was meant to be a means of escaping death produced death on a devastating scale. In the original Naomi is not even mentioned by name, it simply reads, 'The *woman* was bereft of her two sons and husband'. In a passage in which names are linked to personal identity and significance, even that has been lost for Naomi.

Naomi means 'pleasant', maybe reflecting her natural, sweet disposition. But by the time she returns home to Bethlehem she is a changed character entirely: 'When they arrived in Bethlehem, the whole town was stirred because of them, and the women exclaimed, "Can this be Naomi?" "Don't call me Naomi," she told them. "Call me Mara, because the Almighty has made my life very bitter"' (1:19–20). She was scarcely recognizable as the same women who had left those ten long years ago; then she was proud, head held high. Now the cares etched into the lines of her face would have told their own story: this was a women in the abyss of despair, 'empty' – emotionally, spiritually, materially – a woman at the end of her tether. Her life was far from pleasant as her name suggested, it was bitter (*mar*), and she was bitter too. Not necessarily bitterness directed towards God, although there may have been more than an element of that, but there does seem to be a degree of resentment towards herself and her family because of their foolishness and sin resulting in the tragedy they had brought upon themselves.

Naomi did at least recognize that God was present in all of this, in what might be called 'hard providence', 'It is more bitter for me . . . because the LORD's hand has gone out against me' (1:13). However, it was the one whose hand had gone against her that she now reaches out to grasp, because as we read in verse 6 she had heard that the 'LORD had come to the aid of his people'. This is a phrase which resonates with covenant faithfulness. The name, 'Yahweh' too, which appears seven times in chapter 1 alone, is important. It is the covenant name meaning, 'I will be whatever I need to be' for the sake of my people (Exod. 3:14). It is a name which speaks of a love which will not let go, having the long-term interests of his people at heart. And so for Naomi, the one whose hand was against her may yet lift her. So it is to this God, all powerful, all knowing, all loving, she decides to return. The phrase 'return' appears no less than twelve times. It is the same word used by the prophets to call upon Israel to *return* to God; it could easily be rendered 'repent' or 'convert'. So this is not just a physical homecoming for Naomi, it is a spiritual one.

But the Lord had not totally abandoned Naomi, for in his providence he had given her a gem of a daughter-in-law, Ruth:

> But Ruth replied, 'Don't urge me to leave you or to turn back from you. Where you go I will go, and where you stay I will stay. Your people will be my people and your God my God. Where you die I will die, and there I will be buried. May the LORD deal with me, be it ever so severely, if anything but death separates you and me' (1:16–17).

In a book where names mean a lot, so does this name. Ruth means 'friend' and what a wonderful friend she turns out to be.

This is 'covenant language' Ruth is using. It is the kind of language used between God and Israel in the book of Deuteronomy. At the heart of it all is not simply an affectionate loyalty to Naomi, it is a pledge of deep loving service to God and his people. It is a *personal* conversion. Through the quiet, gentle witness of Naomi, Ruth seems to have come to know the one, true and living God. God's ways may be mysterious to us at times, but they are not capricious, he has a loving purpose behind everything he does, as Ruth was to discover to her utter amazement. Even at this stage it would appear that Ruth can see, however dimly, that it is worth forsaking everything in order to know this God. And experience was to prove her right. As we read in verse 22, as they returned, it was 'the beginning of the barley harvest'. That is a telling little phrase not only stating what was the case but acting as a 'cliff hanger', a tantalizing teaser, suggestive of something better to come after the poverty of the famine. With the ending of one episode another begins. As the story unfolds we see how Ruth and Naomi were to enjoy a spiritual harvest, which was eventually to draw people from the four corners of the earth into the orbit of God's saving love.

Even in the first chapter the different strands of God's work in and through all things, are carefully woven together: the providential significance of the names, the severity of God's discipline, the means of converting a pagan, the provision for a lonely widow in repentance and restoration, all of which form a pattern which spell 'unfailing love' (*ḥesed*), a word which appears time and time again throughout the narrative.

But, it is in the second chapter that the pattern of saving love woven by God's providential hand begins to become much clearer, as hard providence gives way to hopeful providence.

Hopeful providence

The entire passage is carefully structured in the original into what is called a *chiasmus,* so that our eyes are draw to the intersecting verse, in which Boaz says to Ruth, 'May the LORD repay you for what you have done. May you be richly rewarded by the LORD, the God of Israel, *under whose wings you have come to take refuge*' (2:12). Like a mother hen gathering her chicks under the protection of her wings to shield them from danger, so God gathers this bereaved, frightened, foreigner to himself (cf. Ps. 36:7, 'How priceless is your unfailing love! Both high and low among men find refuge in the shadow of your wings.').

Our author almost gives the game away right at the beginning of the chapter that something special is about to happen, 'Now Naomi had a relative on her husband's side, from the clan of Elimelech, a man of standing, whose name was Boaz' (2:1). What is so significant about that? Here we have Naomi and Ruth widowed with no children, with the result that there is no-one to care for them. But the all-knowing, all-caring God had made a special provision for such people, it was the institution of the 'kinsmen-redeemer', the *gō'ēl*. This was a tribal society based upon close family ties. Each family or clan had an obligation to defend and provide for other members of the family who were less fortunate than themselves. Such duties extended to providing an heir for a male relative who died childless. It was called the principle of *levirate marriage* (*levir* is the Latin translation of the Hebrew for 'brother-in-law'). According to Deuteronomy 25:5–10, that duty fell on a brother, but it could be extended to a more distant relative who was obliged to marry the widow. The second principle in operation was the *law of redemption* (Lev. 25:25–28), in the buying of a relative's property. The point is this: Boaz was such a relative. So the way is being opened up for the reader to expect a change in fortune such that somewhere along the line this man is going to turn up and things are going to turn out right.

But what guarantee is there that this will happen? God is the guarantee. What he wishes to bring to pass for the good of his people *will* come to pass; he will ensure that it is so. As we have been seeing, there are no 'unknowns' and so no risks for the God of the Bible.

> And Ruth the Moabitess said to Naomi, 'Let me go to the fields and pick up the leftover grain behind anyone in whose eyes I find favour.' Naomi said to her, 'Go ahead, my daughter.' So she went out and began to glean in the fields behind the harvesters. As it turned out, she found herself working in a field belonging to Boaz, who was from the clan of Elimelech. Just then [or, as it 'happened'] Boaz arrived from Bethlehem.

The reader knows that Boaz is a relative, and with Deuteronomy 25 in the background, is aware that there are possibilities here. Ruth ends up in Boaz's field and, lo and behold, just at that moment Boaz turns up! Is this a surprise? Not really, we have already been prepared that something like this might happen. This isn't chance at work with a capital C, but God at work with a capital G, and although Ruth didn't realize this, the reader is on to it and Naomi spotted it straight away:

> Her mother-in-law asked her, 'Where did you glean today? Where did you work? Blessed be the man who took notice of you!' Then Ruth told her mother-in-law about the one at whose place she had been working. 'The name of the man I worked with today is Boaz,' she said. 'The LORD bless him!' Naomi said to her daughter-in-law. 'He has not stopped showing his kindness to the living and the dead.' She added, 'That man is our close relative; he is one of our *kinsman-redeemers*' (2:19–20).

God had been at work superintending and preparing things long before this particular incident occurred, showing he is a God who is gracious. It was because of his laws that Ruth was able to go into the fields picking up the leftover corn in the first place, which then 'just happened' to bring her into contact with her relative-in-law, Boaz. Leviticus 19:9 allowed for the poor to do this, because God cares for the poor. Do you not think that when God instituted such laws of gleaning and redeeming that he didn't *specifically* have Ruth in mind, as well as thousands of other people? After all, he is omniscient. Neither was it an accident that it was to Israel, the only nation on earth which had such laws of grace, that Ruth came, because no other nation worshipped a gracious God whose laws reflected his character. Neither was it accidental that at a time such as this, the time of the judges, which was more or less one of social anarchy, that Ruth was steered (unbeknown to her of course) to a field where her virtue would be protected: 'Naomi said to Ruth her daughter-in-law, "It will be good for you, my daughter, to go with his girls, because in someone else's field you might be harmed"' (2:22). Too true, molestation and rape were common enough in those days. Also do we not think that from the time of his birth, indeed before (because the sort of parents we have affect the people we become), that God was not grooming and shaping the character of Boaz so that he would be the kind and thoughtful man he proved to be (think of Ps. 139)? What is more, we have every good reason to believe that God was working to make him into a prosperous man so that he could provide the material support for Ruth and Naomi which another relative couldn't (as we shall see in ch. 4). The word used to describe Boaz in 2:1 as 'a man of standing' could mean a 'man of wealth' or a 'man of strength' or a 'man of character'. There is every indication as the story unfolds that all three meanings equally applied to Boaz. In other words, he was just the right man, at the right place, at the right time. That is providence, God weaving a purposeful pattern of his own design in our lives

But does this not mean that we become passive fatalists? Not at all, for human responsibility is found in this chapter just as much as divine sovereignty as we see in the actions of the two main characters, Ruth and Boaz.

Let us take the case of Ruth first.

In 2:2 she asks Naomi for permission to go out and do some work. Notice that she doesn't sit back at home moping, 'Woe is me! Let God provide a miracle or two.' She is a woman of faith which means taking action on the basis of what is believed.

First, we see a *humble faith*; look at how she responds to Boaz's kindness, 'At this, she bowed down with her face to the ground. She exclaimed, "Why have I found such favour in your eyes that you notice me – a foreigner?"' (2:10). The word translated 'favour' here and in verse 13 (*ḥēn*) is a word meaning grace. Secondly, it is *selfless faith*. Her reputation as we see in 2:6 is that she is the 'Moabitess who came back from Moab with Naomi', the very thing which Boaz commends her for in verses 11–12. Thirdly, it is an *obedient faith*; she does as Naomi suggests: 'So Ruth stayed close to the servant girls of Boaz to glean until the barley and wheat harvests were finished' (2:23). That is the sort of faith God will always use.

Secondly, we have Boaz.

In the midst of a society in which spiritual rot had set in, Boaz stands out. We notice in 2:4 how he greets his workers, 'The LORD be with you!' This is the sincere blessing of a man who knows his

God. We observe too how he carefully considers Ruth's needs: 'As she got up to glean, Boaz gave orders to his men, "Even if she gathers among the sheaves, don't embarrass her. Rather, pull out some stalks for her from the bundles and leave them for her to pick up, and don't rebuke her"' (2:15–16). Ruth would have been very sensitive to her difference and vulnerability as a Moabite woman on hard times, making her easy prey for abusive men; hence Boaz's keenness to ensure she stays in his field where she would be protected (2:8). What is more, he is generous, 'At meal time Boaz said to her, "Come over here. Have some bread and dip it in the wine vinegar." When she sat down with the harvesters, he offered her some roasted grain. She ate all she wanted and had some left over' (2:14).

In both these people we see how human responsibility plays its part in God achieving his sovereign purposes in the world.

The 'goods' God brings about in our lives are in part a result of the character *we* have been cultivating *under* God. The reason why God could use Boaz as a source of blessing to Ruth and Naomi was because of the kind of man he was. He was a man who knew God's word and lived in its light. Similarly with Ruth. The reason why she commended herself to Boaz was because of the sort of woman she had slowly become. Let me ask: what are you doing to cultivate those virtues which will enable you to respond Christianly when the hard time comes? The only way we will be able to shine when the big tests come our way is by responding well to the little trials as they come our way. Every little thing counts that God uses to make us more into the man or woman of faith he wants us to be.

In this chapter we also see the relationship between God's super-intending grace, active faith and good ends. Some of those 'goods' can be seen in the 'here and now' of the situation, others require a much bigger timescale. There are short-term goods God is bringing about in the life of Ruth as we see in verse 17 where she gathered an ephah, 22 litres of grain, which, frankly, was unheard of. Then there are mid-term goods hinted at in verse 20 that this might be the kinsmen-redeemer who will provide for Ruth and Naomi. But then there is the long-term good which neither Ruth nor Naomi could ever envisage, for as we read at the end of the book in the genealogy, from this most unpromising match, a Moabitess and a landowner, would come King David and nearly a millennium later, Jesus Christ, the Saviour of the world.

Risky business?

The question of timescale is crucial as we turn to chapter 3. Here we discover that three months have passed (the barley and wheat harvests are over) and nothing seems to have happened. Life quietly goes on. Waiting is difficult at the best of times, it is doubly difficult at the worst of times; that is when waiting can so easily turn into restless longing as we impatiently ask the question: Where is God? Why doesn't he *do* something? Here we are back at the central theological message of this book, namely, that of the hidden and active God who *is* continuously at work amongst his people even when it *appears* that nothing is happening. Sometimes God disappears completely into the tapestry of everyday life and we can so easily assume he has forgotten us. But nothing could be further from the truth, he is still at work, perhaps not always in the way we would like or expect, but at work nonetheless. That is something we need to remember especially when we are experiencing the waiting game, the belief that while God may not be prominent he is still present.

That is precisely what Ruth and Naomi are about to discover.

> One day Naomi her mother-in-law said to her, 'My daughter, should I not try to find a home [or 'rest'] for you, where you will be well provided for? Is not Boaz, with whose servant girls you have been, a kinsman of ours? Tonight he will be winnowing barley on the threshing floor. Wash and perfume yourself, and put on your best clothes. Then go down to the threshing floor, but don't let him know you are there until he has finished eating and drinking. When he lies down, note the place where he is lying. Then go and uncover his feet and lie down. He will tell you what to do' (3:1–5).

Imagine the scene: it has been a really hard day. The office has been hectic, the children have been frantic but at last they are safely tucked up in bed, and all the chores have been done. What is the one thing you are looking forward to? Surely, it is rest. According to the Bible rest is one of the greatest blessings God could ever give. That's the blessing Naomi seeks for her daughter-in-law according to verse 1, 'My daughter should I not try to find you *rest*', a better rendering than 'home' as the NIV has it. That one word 'rest' resonates with meaning. In the Scriptures it carries overtones of Eden, when after God created the world he pronounced it very good and he rested. It has associations of harmony, wholeness and peace, resting in the secure knowledge that God is in control.

Far from this being a mere pious hope on the part of Naomi, she takes practical steps to secure it. Certainly this book speaks of God's hand invisibly at work in all the so-called 'coincidences' – providence – but it also emphasizes the part *we* play in acting as responsible agents. Did you notice the feminine planning which went into all of this? First, the right treatment: 'I think a little splash of Chanel 5 wouldn't go amiss tonight my dear,' says Naomi. 'And what about that lovely dress you look so pretty in?' Then second, the right moment, 'Night time is much more romantic than the day. And you need to catch him in the right mood, so go down to the threshing floor, after they have been celebrating the gathering in of the harvest; he is bound to be in good spirits then. But don't let him know you are there until he has finished eating and drinking. When he lies down note the place where he is lying. Then go and uncover his feet, and lie down. He will tell you what to do.' We are not to think that Naomi is being particularly manipulative, in this culture this is just good old-fashioned common sense.

Ruth does precisely what she was told:

> So she went down to the threshing floor and did everything her mother-in-law told her to do. When Boaz had finished eating and drinking and was in good spirits, he went over to lie down at the far end of the grain

pile. Ruth approached quietly, uncovered his feet and lay down. In the middle of the night something startled the man, and he turned and discovered a woman lying at his feet. 'Who are you?' he asked. 'I am your servant Ruth,' she said. 'Spread the corner of your garment over me, since you are a kinsman-redeemer' (3:6–9).

You have to give Ruth full marks for courage, if not outright audacity. Can you imagine the enormous risk she was taking? By approaching this man in the pitch dark she was gambling not only with her dignity but her chastity as she lay at his feet, which in this culture is the place of submission. If he chose to take sexual advantage of the situation she would have no defence.

But faith, by definition, involves an element of risk otherwise it wouldn't be faith. Of course this is not the reckless risk of a teenage joy rider; it is the calculated risk of someone who knows God. She enters that barn trusting that she is under the divine protective wings of refuge. She has heard of the promises of the Lord, she has already experienced something of his gracious provision as we saw back in chapter 2. The signs look favourable, *but* one hundred per cent success is not guaranteed beforehand. That is where faith comes in.

It is in Ruth's request that we really see her launch out in expectant faith, 'I am your servant Ruth, spread the corner of your garment over me, since you are a kinsman-redeemer' (3:9b). What Ruth is saying is deliberately ambiguous. On the one hand the phrase in Hebrew can be taken to mean 'marry me'. To 'spread the corner of your garment' is a little like a woman today asking for an engagement ring to be placed on her finger. We see this figure of speech being used in Ezekiel 16:8 to describe God acting like a lover towards Israel, 'I saw that you were old enough for love, I spread the corner of my garment over you and covered your nakedness'. To 'cover with one's cloak' spoke of affording protection, providing the 'rest' or 'home' (3:1) which a woman needs. On the other hand, the word for 'garment' is the same word used in 2:12 for 'wings': 'spread your wings over me', the 'wings of God's refuge' which Boaz commended

Ruth for seeking. Ruth could therefore in effect be saying, 'You prayed for my blessing Boaz, since I sought the protective wings of the Lord. Well, you are my dead husband's relative, a kinsman-redeemer. Shouldn't you do more than pray for me? You have a responsibility under God's law to provide for me. Don't you see Boaz, you could be the answer to your own prayer? Maybe God is calling *you* to be the protective wings he wants to spread over me.' True piety is always practical.

Ruth's faith is then rewarded:

> 'The LORD bless you, my daughter,' he replied. 'This kindness is greater than that which you showed earlier: You have not run after the younger men, whether rich or poor. And now, my daughter, don't be afraid. I will do for you all you ask. All my fellow townsmen know that you are a woman of noble character.'

Boaz understood perfectly what she was saying and was impressed by her motives and devotion, especially her kindness to Naomi in wishing to provide a male heir for the family, and the kindness (*ḥesed*) to himself when she could have sought a much younger man. For a woman like this he will do anything to redeem her (3:13). Maybe not anything, because there is one fly in the ointment, there was another relative who was a closer kinsman-redeemer and so legally had first call on the situation: 'Although it is true that I am near of kin, there is a kinsman-redeemer who is more closely related than I' (3:12). Boaz was determined to do God's work, God's way. There was no question of him trying to take a short cut by casting God's law to one side. No, he too would have to trust in God and his providence. Here we see Boaz submitting to the kind of guidance we looked at in an earlier chapter. He knew God's moral law and was sticking to that. He also trusted in God's sovereignty, but as the final chapter shows, there is an area of freedom in which he can move, using wisdom to bring about a desired goal, a kind of redemption, but not at the expense of disobeying God.

God works for the good

At the beginning of chapter 4 we have a 'will he or won't he?' situation. Will Boaz be able to enter into marriage with Ruth and secure the family land or does the existence of a closer relative throw his (and God's) plans into jeopardy?

It would not be difficult to imagine that if word got out to this other relative that Boaz had designs on Ruth, it would raise the negotiating stakes considerably. The unnamed relative could drive a hard bargain, playing on Boaz's emotions. This has to be handled with tremendous cool and diplomacy. And so in a carefully planned, but apparently 'accidental' meeting, the other relative turns up at the gate of the city, the place where matters of business and finance were conducted. Wisely Boaz doesn't mention Ruth at all, he speaks solely in terms of property.

> Then he said to the kinsman-redeemer, 'Naomi, who has come back from Moab, is selling the piece of land that belonged to our relative Elimelech. I thought I should bring the matter to your attention and suggest that you buy it in the presence of these seated here and in the presence of the elders of my people. If you will redeem it, do so. But if you will not, tell me, so I will know. For no one has the right to do it except you, and I am next in line' (3:3–4).

Naomi's dead husband held some property that according to Israelite law passed on to the next of kin, this unnamed relative. But there were the needs of the widow to consider. She would have to be provided for, and in this sense perhaps, Boaz speaks of her as 'selling the land', not that she had a right to do so, but morally there should be some revenue from the land which would support her in her need. So far, so good. The relative reflects on this and considers it a good deal. After all, Naomi is old and therefore will not have any more children to whom the property would automatically be transferred. So, yes he could give Naomi some money and he in the meantime he will have extended his own real estate. That is when

Boaz drops the bombshell. 'Oh, you do realize that there is someone else, Ruth the Moabitess.' One could imagine him emphasizing her pedigree. Not only is there the law in Leviticus to consider about redeeming property, but also the associated law in Deuteronomy about marriage and offspring (4:5). Naomi may be past child-bearing age, but Ruth certainly isn't.

So it may not be such a good deal after all: 'At this the kinsman-redeemer said; "Then I cannot redeem it because I might endanger my own estate. You redeem it yourself. I cannot do it"' (4:6). The relative may now realize that if he marries Ruth and she has a son, then the land automatically reverts to her son, in which case he loses both the money he has laid out in his initial investment *and* the land. This was one price this man was not willing to pay.

Not so Boaz. He was willing to take on all the responsibilities in providing for these two desperate women. What is more, he was going to be seen to be above board about it all, hence all this business about exchanging sandals, the equivalent to a signature at the bottom of a contract, in full view of witnesses.

The story has a triple climax. There is blessing for Ruth and Boaz in verses 11 and 13: 'May the LORD make the woman who is coming into your home like Rachel and Leah, who together built up the house of Israel. . . . So Boaz took Ruth and she became his wife . . . and she gave birth to a son.' There is blessing for Naomi: 'Then Naomi took the child, laid him in her lap and cared for him. The women living there said, "Naomi has a son"' (4:16). But then there is a blessing which far outstrips them all: 'And they named him Obed. He was the father of Jesse, the father of David' (4:17). This is how Israel, and the whole world, was to have a King.

As Naomi looked into the face of that little Jewish baby she had no idea that she was holding not only the one who was to be *her* kinsmen-redeemer, but the one whose descendent would be *the* kinsmen-redeemer of the whole human race, *the* Servant of the Lord (this is what the name Obadiah means) *par excellence*, the Lord Jesus Christ. This genealogy selectively traces the royal line. Perez (4:12, 18) is the son of Judah from whom the Messiah was to come

(Gen. 49:10). That is where the genealogy is leading to with David, Ruth's grandson.

However, this story needs to be placed within the grand sweep of Scripture as it forms one small, but highly significant episode in the drama of redemption. This is what Matthew does in the New Testament. In his Gospel he takes this genealogy and incorporates it in the family tree which opens his book: the family tree of Jesus. There are, however, two modifications Matthew makes. He explicitly links Boaz with Ruth his wife and Rahab his mother (Matt. 1:5). What is significant about that? As we have seen Ruth began life as a Moabite, a pagan. Rahab began life as a Canaanite and a harlot. A pagan and a prostitute are embedded in the family tree of God's Holy Son! At the very least this tells us that God's salvation is universal in scope (embracing Gentiles and Jews) and specific in effect, individual people are in view, a Rahab, a Ruth, a Kim Phuc.

The story of Ruth is in many ways a paradigm story of God's wise and inscrutable providence. Unless God's knowledge of the future was exhaustive and infallible, and his ability to work in and through all things (including human decisions freely made), then the story simply wouldn't work. Over all the detail God's sovereignty extends. God's providence is seen in the provision of his law for the widow (levirate marriage) and the hungry (gleaning the barley fields), which had they not been in operation, or had operated differently, would not have resulted in this story being in the Bible. God's providence is seen in the hard place of Elimelech's family disobediently leaving the land of promise by divine permission (while still contrary to his revealed will), but with the good end that Ruth becomes a follower of Yahweh, outshining many of the native Israelites in her godliness (God intended *this* for good). It is seen in the detail of Ruth finding herself in one field rather than another. Had that not happened, the encounter with Boaz would not have materialized, and again the story would not have been told. But the whole interconnectedness of God's providence extends not only backwards in time but forwards, gathering up *all* the details of human history, in order for the true *gō'ēl* kinsmen-redeemer to come, the Lord Jesus Christ: 'But when the time had fully come, God sent his Son, born of a woman, born under the law, to redeem those under the law' (Gal. 4:5). The story of Ruth embraced the detail of the exact place where all this took place, Bethlehem. And so for the prophecy of the Messiah's birth to be fulfilled (Mic. 5:2; Matt. 2:5), God's providential rule had to extend not only over this episode, involving this family, but also including the order of a pagan emperor calling for a census (Luke 2:1–7). In short, without the no-risk doctrine of providence illustrated by the story of Ruth and testified to throughout the Bible, salvation itself would be threatened. But as we have seen, no such threat does or can exist. The apostle Paul's words remain steadfast and clear:

> And we know that in all things God works for the good of those who love him, who have been called according to his purpose. For those God foreknew he also predestined to be conformed to the image of his Son, that he might be the firstborn among many brothers and sisters. And those he predestined, he also called; those he called, he also justified; those he justified, he also glorified (Rom. 8:28–30, TNIV).

Questions for reflection and discussion

1. Think back over all the different areas of life that God's providence touches that we have considered (e.g. prayer, action, conversion). How do you see each one in the story of Ruth?
2. In what ways have you tried to take matters into your own hands, like Elimelech, without trusting God's providence wholeheartedly?
3. How does God's providence help us to be action-taking, risk-taking men and women like Ruth and Boaz?
4. What does the book of Ruth tell about God's providence in sending our redeemer, Jesus?

5. 'May you be richly rewarded by the LORD, the God of Israel, under whose wings you have come to take refuge.' How will this picture change how you view God and his providence?

6. Spend some time reflecting on all that God has taught you from his word about his providence. What do you need to repent of and ask for change for? What does God deserve your praise and worship for?

APPENDIX: GOING DEEPER

The author of Ecclesiastes makes a poignant observation when he writes, 'Of making many books there is no end, and much study wearies the body' (12:12). We may feel that saying particularly applies to the subject of God's sovereignty and providence!

The position I have been taking throughout this volume can be described as the 'classic Reformed view' and stands in the tradition of scholars like Augustine and Calvin. Obviously there are many related philosophical and theological issues we have not been able to deal with, but footnotes have been provided so that readers can follow up some of these issues for themselves. Instead, there has been an attempt to expound biblical material in a way which has a positive pastoral application. However, in this appendix I wish to draw attention to alternative views of providence which attempt to wrestle with the biblical material and then to offer a few reflections.

In his book, *Providence and Prayer*, Terrance Tiessen considers ten models of providence and offers one of his own.[1] This is an excellent

resource for anyone wishing to consider the strengths and weaknesses of the different models which are in the theological world.
Tiessen's treatment is always fair, judicious and clear. For our
purposes, however, I shall restrict myself to two other views, which,
in varying degrees, are popular.

The Arminian-Molinist view

This is represented by William Lane Craig, as for example in the
book, *Four Views of Divine Providence*.[2]

'Molinism' refers to a view of God's knowledge and his relation
to the world which has its origins in the sixteenth century. The name
is derived from a Jesuit theologian, Luis de Molina. Following
Molina, Craig argues that there are three types of knowledge in God:
natural, free, and middle knowledge. Prior to the divine decree to
create the actual world we know, God possesses what is referred
to as 'natural knowledge', that is, he knows the range of all things
that 'could happen', all possible worlds if you will, or in the words
of Craig, 'God had knowledge of all necessary truths, including all
the possible worlds he might create'.[3] In addition to this he possesses
what is called 'middle knowledge', such that he knows all possible
feasible worlds and what 'would' happen in such worlds. The things
that 'could' or 'would' happen in such alternative hypothetical worlds
are called 'counterfactuals'. It is when God carries out his creative
decree that he knows the actual world; this is called 'free knowledge',
those things which God has freely planned to bring to pass. This
means, according to Craig, that 'logically subsequent to his decree
to create a particular world, God knows all the contingent truths
about the actual world, including its past, present, and future'.[4]

Armed with these distinctions, Craig argues that we are in a
position to affirm God's sovereignty and omniscience and a libertarian view of freedom. 'Not only does this view make room for human
freedom, but it affords God a means of choosing which world of
free creatures to create. For by knowing how persons would freely

choose in whatever circumstances they might be, God can, by decreeing to place just those persons in just those circumstances, bring about his ultimate purposes *through* free creaturely decisions. Thus, by employing his hypothetical knowledge, God can plan a world down to the last detail and yet do so without annihilating creaturely freedom, since God has already factored into the equation what people would do freely under various circumstances.'[5]

Craig cites biblical support for his position. For example, Jesus affirms before Pilate the counterfactual conditional: 'Jesus said, "My kingdom is not of this world. If it were, my servants would fight to prevent my arrest by the Jews. But now my kingdom is from another place"' (John 18:36). The Scriptures, it is argued, abound with examples of such counterfactual conditionals concerning creaturely choices and actions (one may also think of Jesus' statement: 'Woe to you, Korazin! Woe to you, Bethsaida! If the miracles that were performed in you had been performed in Tyre and Sidon, they would have repented long ago in sackcloth and ashes', Matt. 11:21).

Appeal to such texts does not decide the question of whether God possesses middle knowledge however, which Craig himself admits:

> Biblically speaking, it is not difficult to show that God possesses hypothetical knowledge. For example, Jesus affirms before Pilate the counterfactual conditional 'If my kingship were of this world, my servants would fight, that I might not be handed over to the Jews' (John 18:36, RSV). The Scriptures abound with examples of such counterfactual conditionals concerning creaturely choices and actions. Unfortunately, this fact does not settle the matter of whether God has middle knowledge. For the scriptural passages show only that God possesses knowledge of counterfactual propositions, and, as I have said, until modern times all theologians agreed that God possesses such hypothetical knowledge. The question remains, when in the logical order of things does this knowledge come? Is it before or after the divine decree? Since Scripture does not reflect on this question, no amount of proof texting concerning God's hypothetical knowledge can prove that such knowledge is possessed logically prior to God's creative decree. This

is a matter for theologico-philosophical reflection, not biblical exegesis. Thus, while it is clearly unbiblical to deny that God has hypothetical knowledge, those who deny middle knowledge while affirming God's hypothetical knowledge cannot be accused of being unbiblical.'[6]

In his presentation, Craig sidesteps the biblical material which underscores God's absolute sovereignty over human agents and focuses instead on the philosophical arguments (presumably because on his own admission there are not that many passages which point in the direction of middle knowledge).

I shall make three observations.

First, in the classic Reformed tradition, passages such as John 18:36 and Matthew 11:21 and following, would be considered part of God's *natural knowledge* (that God knows all possibilities simply because he is all knowing). This is consistent with the notion of freedom known as voluntarism, and so is part of the compatibilist position. There is no need to appeal to 'middle knowledge', indeed, it can be argued that it is not possible to do so.[7]

Secondly, Craig's position assumes a libertarian view of freedom which is far from being proven to be one which the Bible writers would agree with.[8]

Thirdly, we may question whether Molinism's middle-knowledge is capable of holding together libertarian freedom and God's sovereignty. It is difficult to see how, if God has actual knowledge of what someone would do in various hypothetical worlds, this is any different to God's natural knowledge, in which case libertarian freedom is compromised. Or to put it another way, if taking a strong libertarian line, man always has the ability to do otherwise whatever hypothetical world he is in, then God cannot know what choice he will make because for God to know such a choice with certainty would mean that man is not free to do otherwise. This is because God's certainty eliminates such a choice. On the other hand, no matter how many hypothetical worlds there are, if man is always free to act to the contrary in such worlds, then God's knowledge is limited and his sovereignty compromised.

The Open Theism view

This has been referred to on a number of occasions throughout this book together with its main protagonists, Clark Pinnock, John Sanders and Gregory Boyd. For the purposes of this section we shall take Gregory Boyd as representative as we find his presentation in the same volume as Craig's entitled, 'God Limits His Control'.[9]

There are five foundational pillars which form the basis for this view.

First, divine, universal, egalitarian love and libertarian freedom are non-negotiable. Because God is a loving God and wishes to have a loving relationship with the creatures he has made, libertarian freedom is essential, it is argued, for that love to be reciprocal, otherwise we are mere puppets: 'He must give us genuine say-so to affect what comes to pass as we choose lovingly to align our wills with his or not.'[10]

Secondly, since God created us to have the freedom to love or not love him, God has made himself 'vulnerable', capable of being rejected and grieved. In other words, God does not always get what he wants or what he wills but we often thwart his intended plans.

Thirdly, by virtue of wanting to create this kind of world, God cannot control what human beings do:

> God's decision to create a cosmos that was capable of love and that was, therefore, populated with free agents was also a decision to create and govern a world he could not unilaterally control. . . . What it means for God to give agents some degree of morally responsible say-so over what comes to pass is that God's say-so will not unilaterally determine all that comes to pass.[11]

Boyd goes on to write:

> I and other open theists thus hold that God limits the exercise of his power when he creates free agents. To the extent that God gives an agent free will, he *cannot* meticulously control what that agent does. Yet the

'cannot' in this statement is not a matter of insufficient power, for God remains all-powerful. It rather is simply a matter of definition. Just as God cannot create a round triangle or a married bachelor, so too he cannot meticulously control free agents.[12]

The 'cannot' of which Boyd speaks is a 'logical cannot' and as such does not bring into question God's omnipotence.

Fourthly (and this is what has given rise to the name of this school of thought), the future is open as much to God as it is to his creatures. God knows various possibilities of what might happen but is not in a position to know what a person will do, however, once things are actualized then he can be responsive. Thus God's knowledge of the future is limited and not exhaustive. Such limited knowledge, it is argued, is necessary to preserve libertarian freedom.

Fifthly and finally, because the future is open to both us and to God, our life on earth is like a 'Choose Your Own Adventure' book, whereby the reader follows a narrative through and at critical points can choose from several alternatives what to do next.

To summarize in Boyd's own words, 'The open model argues that God does not meticulously control everything precisely because God is a God of perfect love. God's other-orientated greatness was displayed when, out of love, God limited the exercise of his power by granting agents their own domain of morally responsible say-so.'[13]

Open theism has been subject to extensive criticism over the years;[14] here I will draw attention to some of the most serious concerns and weaknesses.

First, there is a basic problem of method. Certainly in the case of Boyd it is not a matter of approaching what Scripture has to say on such matters as divine sovereignty, human responsibility, the existence of evil and suffering and inductively attempting to formulate a coherent theology. Instead it is a question of beginning with experience and then trying to fit Scripture in with that. So Boyd confesses that he finds views where 'God determines the free choices of agents' to be unable to 'to ascribe coherent meaning to it'. The reason given is, 'I find nothing in my experience – or any conceivable experience – that sheds the least bit of light on what this mysterious "in such a way" (speaking of determinist models) . . . might mean.'[15] The primacy of experience shaping his approach is even more evident in his book, *God of the Possible*[16] and the case of 'Suzanne'. While experience and particular pastoral matters might cause us to seek what Scripture has to say on such matters, it is not the case that such matters determine what Scriptures *can* say.

Secondly, it is difficult not to conclude that the God of open theism is other than the God of the Bible and so no god at all. Open theism simply does not do justice to the vast reams of biblical passages which present God as all knowing and all powerful, texts such as Isaiah 40 – 66 (God's exhaustive knowledge of the future is put forward as a distinguishing feature over the false gods who know no such things, Isa. 41:21–29), let alone the whole book of Revelation. The open theists have constructed a 'procrustean bed' such that whichever passages do not fit with their scheme are effectively lopped off.

The 'no god' we are left with is not simply a risk taker, but an irresponsible mad-scientist who, Dr Frankenstein-like, starts out full of good intentions, but brings into being creatures in such a way that things get hopelessly out of control. And although he is trying to do his best to tame the beast, for the sake of 'love' he cannot guarantee a good outcome; he must run the risk of being endlessly frustrated. This effectively shelves the biblical notion of hope (what does one do with texts like Rom. 8:28ff?). On this view, protestations notwithstanding, there is no final assurance of the victory of God.

Boyd would certainly contest this claim as he draws upon an illustration of Peter Geach which represents God as a chess Grand Master pitted against a novice, who represents human freedom. Since the Grand Master has sufficient skill, whatever moves his opponent makes, he will outmanoeuvre him and eventually win the game.[17]

However, it is difficult to see how the Grand Master analogy fits with libertarian freedom. Surely, libertarian freedom necessitates that the 'novice' need not play by the rules of the game? If he so chose, he could move his rook diagonally or his king six places instead of one. According to the libertarian view of freedom, although there are limitations imposed, the world of human affairs is not such a closed and predictable system as a game of chess. The 'end game' is far from secure.[18]

This leads to the next weakness, namely, far from this position easing the 'problem of evil' (and any attempt to understand the oceans of human suffering that have existed) it intensifies it. For not only, as we have seen, is one logically compelled to conceive of God as acting irresponsibly in bringing into existence a creation in which he can exercise no effective control to determine a successful outcome, but it raises the question of whether the 'trade off' is justified. The alleged benefit of having unmitigated evil and untold misery (which includes the suffering of hell), is that we can exercise a certain kind of freedom. Many would question that. Neither is it the case, as argued by open theists, that potential evil must exist to exercise human freedom, for where does this leave God's freedom? Either God is not free because potential evil is not an option for him or if God is able to be free without the possibility of evil, then why not human beings?[19]

Of course responses have been made to such objections[20] and readers may wish to investigate these for themselves. But in our opinion, this position is particularly to be found wanting.

Notes

1. Terrance Tiessen, *Providence and Prayer – How Does God Work in the World?* (InterVarsity Press, 2000).

2. *Four Views on Divine Providence*, ed. Stanley N. Gundry (Zondervan, 2011).

3. Craig, in *Four Views*, pp. 80-81.

4. Craig, in *Four Views*, p. 81.

5. Craig, in *Four Views*, p. 82.

6. Craig, in *Four Views*, pp. 83–84.

7. Tiessen's model mentioned above, in *Providence and Prayer*, is an attempt to consider providence in terms of middle-knowledge and compatibilism, which has been strongly contested by Paul Helm and shown not to be feasible. This has been accepted by Tiessen and as a result he has withdrawn his proposal in Paul Helm and Terrance Tiessen, 'Does Calvinism Have Room For Middle-Knowledge? A Conversation', *Westminster Journal of Theology* 71 (2009), pp. 437–454.

8. 'Reformed believers suggest not only that libertarian freedom is impossible to reconcile with many of the things that Scripture explicitly teaches about God's relationship to the things that "hold together" (Col. 1:17) and have their "being" (Acts 17:28) in him, but also that the concept of libertarian freedom is itself extremely problematic, for it presumes that "some things existed prior to and apart from the creative work of God and continue to exist outside of God's providence"' (Paul Helseth, 'God Causes All Things', in Gundry (ed.), *Four Views*, pp. 41–43). See also John Frame, *The Doctrine of God – A Theology of Lordship* (P. & R. Publishing, 2002), p. 140ff, where he provides eighteen objections to the libertarian notion of freedom.

9. Gregory Boyd, 'God Limits His Control', in Gundry, *Four Views*.

10. Boyd, in *Four Views*, p. 189.

11. Boyd, in *Four Views*, p. 190.

12. Boyd, in *Four Views*, p. 191.

13. Boyd, in *Four Views*, p. 204.

14. Gerald Bray, *The Personal God: Is the Classical Understanding of God Tenable?* (Paternoster Press, 1998); Bruce A. Ware, *God's Lesser Glory: A Critique of Open Theism* (Apollos, 2001); John M. Frame, *No Other God: A Response to Open Theism* (P. & R. Publishing, 2001); Steven C. Roy, *How Much Does God Foreknow? A Comprehensive Biblical Study* (Apollos, 2006).

15. Boyd, in *Four Views*, p. 190.

16. Gregory A. Boyd, *God of the Possible. A Biblical Introduction to the Open View of God* (Baker, 2000), p. 104.

17. Peter Geach, *Providence and Evil* (Cambridge University Press, 1977), p. 58; Gregory Boyd, *Satan and the Problem of Evil: Constructing a Trinitarian Warfare Theodicy* (InterVarsity Press, 2001), p. 113.

18. 'How can we be sure that God will triumph over (evil) in the end? Of course, God *says* in Scripture that he will triumph over evil. But if he was unable to keep it out of his universe in the first place and it came in against his will, and if he is unable to predict the outcome of any future events that involve the free choices by human, angelic and demonic agents, how then can we be sure that God's declaration that he will triumph over all evil is itself true? Perhaps this is just a hopeful prediction of something that . . . God cannot know' (Wayne Grudem, *Systematic Theology* [Inter-Varsity Press, 1994], p. 350).

19. '. . . The God of open theism is not as distant from responsibility for evil as it is claimed. He knows every plan as it unfolds and can certainly anticipate evil decisions that are coming. He possesses the right to intervene unilaterally but in the vast majority of cases chooses not to. Thus the evils in the world occur because God specifically permitted them to happen – though there is no greater good that would justify them. In short, he is intimately involved in the occurrence of evil' (Roy, *How Much Does God Foreknow?*, p. 264).

20. See Gundry (ed.), *Four Views*; Bruce A. Ware (ed.), *Perspectives on the Doctrine of God: Four Views* (B & H Academic, 2008).